My Three Countries

A JOURNEY FROM PRIVILEGE TO SLAVERY TO FREEDOM

ANNA MELGAARD

**As told to Ellie Fredricks,
Alice (Melgaard) Ard and Mandy Melgaard**

MY THREE COUNTRIES

ISBN 978-1-54393-518-9 (print)s
ISBN: 978-1-54393-519-6 (ebook)

CONTENTS

PART I
ROMANIA

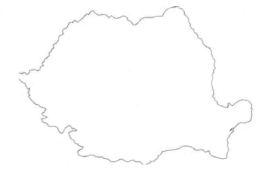

CHAPTER 1

A Little History

E xcept for my accent and my penchant for hard work, no one would guess that I once lived through some very harrowing and uncertain years far, far away from Prosser, Washington.

My name is Anna Untch Melgaard. I'm German, even though I was born and raised in Reichesdorf, Romania. To explain this, let me tell you the history of the land that people call Transylvania, "the land beyond the forest."

Roman Heritage

Down through the ages, many different peoples and cultures found Transylvania to be a desirable place to live. It had fertile lands, rich natural resources, and was the juncture of major trading routes. Nations fought over the region for its gold, salt, and other minerals.

Between 101 and 106 AD, Rome controlled Transylvania. They built roads, bridges, and a great wall for protection. These new roads facilitated trade with other Roman provinces. Latin became the official language.

The Romans fended off invasions by the Huns, Avars, Slavs, and Bulgars, but the Goths proved too strong and the Romans had to drop back to the Danube River. Some however, chose to stay in Transylvania. They were the ancestors of modern day Romanians. Their Latin evolved into today's Romanian language.

An Invitation from Hungary

In 895AD, the Magyars (Hungarians) conquered Transylvania. King Stephen I of Hungary, crowned in 1000AD, made the region a Catholic principality. He wanted hardy and industrous settlers to colonize the land, secure the borders, and convert the pagans. In order to entice people to risk immigrating to such a remote place, he promised security, liberty, and chances for advancements and higher rank. Many Europeans, oppressed under the feudal system, saw the opportunities King Stephen I offered as the only chance they would ever have to own land; and to have political, economic, and religious independence. They began immigrating to Transylvania, a distance of over one thousand miles, in the middle of the 12th century and continued on and off for more than a hundred years.

King Geysa II (1142-1162) was particularly successful in attracting German and Flemish farmers, tradesmen, and lower nobility to settle in Transylvania. He offered the "Hungarian

Right of Hospitality" to all the people he invited to his empire, promising plenty of fertile land and complete autonomy to elect their own officials and ministers. In 1224, his successor, Andrew II, wrote these privileges down in the "Guarantee of Freedom," spelling out sixteen freedoms, which were honored for many centuries. These freedoms allowed the "German guests" to make their own laws and to elect their own judges to settle disputes. The immigrants had open access to Transylvania's natural resources, including forests and water. German tradesmen could travel freely throughout the kingdom. Their markets were not taxed and they could worship as they wished.

My Ancestors Accept the Invitation

Conditions in Germany were very bad in the 1100s. After three consecutive wars, the people had nothing to sell and no money to pay taxes. My ancestors and others leapt at King Geysa's invitation and fled their oppression to settle virgin territories in "the land beyond the forest." They hauled everything they could on wagons drawn by oxen.

It took many weeks of marching across Germany and Slavish provinces to reach the Hungarian border. My ancestors trudged through rivers, swamps, and dangerous stretches of sand. They risked encounters with bears, boars, wolves, bison, and other wild animals. The sparse groups living in these regions were savage and hostile. They attacked the travelers, taking their possessions, killing men, and violating women.

Once in Hungary, the groups were guided by a commissioner of King Geysa II. They followed him until he finally halted the wagon train on a hill. He swept his hand south and east and exclaimed, "Friends, stretching far and wide before you, you see your new homeland!" The immigrants saw endless forest-covered hills and mountains, broad valleys, numerous rivers, and sparkling lakes. The land was rich and beautiful, leaving some people speechless. It was also wild and lonesome, leaving others disillusioned and bitter.

For decades, individuals and family after family left the Rhine and Mosel River valleys to settle in Transylvania.

Securing Their New Land

My forefathers and fellow settlers chose sites for villages, and then worked diligently to tame the land. In 1283, the community leaders drew up land divisions, allotting my home town of Reichesdorf 4,500 *Joch*, about 6,345 acres. These acres were so productive that, in 1359, the little village paid 14 *Mark* in taxes, equal to a half pound of silver.

Of their numerous enemies, the settlers most dreaded the Cumans from central Asia. Our people fought a bloody battle against them. Many were killed and still more enslaved. Eventually, the settlers overtook and completely defeated the Cumans. They freed the captives, but mourned great losses. These brave and hardy Germans did not weaken or leave the country, though. On the contrary, new immigrants continued to arrive. They built strong castles and dug deep moats around them. Seven such castles were built, and from them, legend says, the country received its name, *Siebenburgen*, "Seven Castles."

A New Identity: "Transylvania Saxons" – The Privileged

Besides our people, from northern and middle Germany, others also came to Transylvania from the western regions of what was then Germany, and from Luxembourg, Flanders, Bavaria, Thüringen, and Saxony. Hungary granted all of the settlers many freedoms. Over time, documents came to refer to anyone who had these special rights as "Saxons." "Saxon" was, therefore, a synonym for legal status with privileges, not simply a name of origin. Because of their Western European heritage and connections, Saxons tended to have higher education, political savvy and economic status than the more numerous ethnic citizens of Transylvania, the Romanians.

The "Transylvanian Saxons" developed their designated lands quickly. They not only made the soil arable and improved agricultural methods, but they also mined the precious metals in the Carpathian Mountains and the salt deposits in the Transylvanian Plateau. In addition, they advanced handicrafts and trade.

In 1370, they built a wall across the mountain pass to keep enemies out, mostly Turks. Later, as more and more enemies tried to enter, the Saxons constructed walls around their churches. In the 1400s, each village housed a big, walled-in church, where people could run for protection when enemies encroached. Men could pour hot tar on attackers through openings at the top of the wall. Reichesdorf built its church and wall in 1451. These churches also had big towers, which doubled as lookouts and had bells to ring out warnings when invaders threatened. In order to be close to their churches, Saxons lived in their villages and not on their land (like people do in the United States.) The church was the pride of the villagers; the governing, social, and spiritual center of their lives; and the strongest of all organizations. Saxons were God-fearing, honest, and hardworking people.

Devastating Invasions

In the 1600s, the Turks invaded and plundered Transylvania, burning down homes and taking all they could with them. They stayed in Reichesdorf for ten weeks. The Reichesdorf minister, who had lost his whole family to disease, wrote that he didn't know what to fear more, disease or Turks.

From 1703 to 1711, the Kurutzen [Hungarian rebel crusaders] raged wars in Transylvania. They plundered and pillaged the villages. Of the 152 families in Reichesdorf, at the beginning of 1690, only 43 remained in 1720. To help the Saxons get back on their feet, the Evangelical Church in Germany sent money and books.

A Neighbor Country, Romania, Is Born

After the Russo-Turkish War of 1828 – 1829, the Russians became a major power in the region. In 1877, after another war against the Turks in which Russia enlisted the help of Romania, the Turks' reign ended. In 1878, Romania achieved full independence as a country, including the regions of Moldavia, Walachia, and Dobruja (acquired from Bulgaria.) Russia gained Bessarabia. Transylvania remained a part of Austria-Hungary.

Romania Gains Transylvania

In 1916, Romania joined the WWI Allies (mostly Russia, Italy, France, and Great Britain) in their fight against Austria-Hungary and Germany. The allies won in 1918 and Romania gained Transylvania as part of the peace settlement. With Transylvania, Romania almost doubled its area and population.

The Saxons, however, remained firmly devoted to their German roots. Very seldom did any of them mix with non-Germans. They had their own German-speaking churches and schools. Saxon graduates of secondary schools set out for Protestant universities in Germany. Centuries of trade and commerce also reinforced these ties to their motherland.

In a letter to the Frankfurt National Assembly in the mid-1800s, a large group of Saxon youth put together a very comprehensive statement:

> *The world is filled with German children. We too are descendants of these roots. Geographically separated and on the surface without visible bonds to the motherland, still, we live through the press, through*

the universities, through the travels of our tradesmen, through memories of the past and the hopes of the future with and through Germany.... We are strong if Germany is strong.... We want to be and remain what we have always been, an honest German people and also honest and loyal citizens of the country we belong to.

Racism and Discontent

Romania guaranteed all groups in Transylvania "full ethnic freedom for the fellow citizens." They confirmed, by contract, protection for all minorities regarding equal rights, political representation, religious and cultural autonomy, independent school systems, and freedom to speak their native language.

Unfortunately, these protections were rarely followed. The Romanian constitution of 1923 hardly mentioned the Saxon protections. Romanians used continual land reforms to further erode the Saxon's rights. In efforts to redistribute wealth and promote equality among its citizens, the Romanian government took land and businesses from the wealthier minority ethnicities, (such as the Saxons, Hungarians, and Jews) and parceled them out to the poorer Romanians, or kept them under government control.

The Transylvanian Saxons believed in a democratic society, where "nobody is master and nobody is servant," and where citizens can elect their own political and clerical representatives. So, in the 1920s, Saxons and other German groups in the country banded together to form the Alliance of Germans in Romania. This brought few improvements, however. To add to German discontent, in1929 Romania's economy plunged in the world-wide economic crisis. High unemployment and political unrest led to the rapid growth of fascist organizations. Romania slowly slipped under the influence of Nazi Germany. The government instituted rigid censorship and ruled by decree. As a result, radical nationalistic oriented groups popped up among the traditional Transylvanian Saxons.

Nazism

From 1930 to 1940, while I was growing up, King Carol II [Romanian for "Charles II"] ruled Romania. After several scandalous affairs, he abdicated the throne to his son, Michael, who was still a minor. Marshal Ion Antonescu, supported by the German government, stepped in and took control of the Romanian People's Republic.

The Saxons grew more and more attracted to Hitler's National Socialism policy, with horrendous consequences. Hitler's government in Germany used the Alliance of Germans in Romania to increase its influence in Romania. "Saxon" received the stamp of "German Messenger." Anyone who didn't go along with Nazi Germany's agenda was replaced. In 1940, a territorial dispute, arbitrated by Nazi Germany and Fascist Italy, divided Transylvania. Northern Transylvania went to Hungary; Southern Transylvania (which included Reichesdorf) remained with Romania.

The German government intervened more and more openly in matters of the Saxons, leading to 1943, when the Romanians agreed that their citizens of Germanic heritage be required to serve in the German military forces, especially, the Waffen-SS, to fight in World War II. Transylvanian Saxons served in three armies during WWII: the older Saxons of Southern Transylvania served in the Romanian army, the older Northern Transylvanian Saxons served in the Hungarian army, and all the younger Saxons served in the German forces.

Surrender

Toward the end of WWII, when the Soviet army advanced into Romania and bombed the transportation systems, Romania surrendered to the Allies (to USSR, France, Britain, and the U.S., among others). On August 23, 1944, the Romanian government signed a truce with their enemies and then about-faced and declared war on its previous allies (Germany, Italy, Hungary…) Artur Phleps, a Transylvanian Saxon and General in the German army, realized how desperate and dangerous this situation was for his countrymen in Romania. He ordered the evacuation of the Saxons in the Nosnerland of Northern Transylvania. Many escaped to Austria. The Saxons in Southern Transylvania (my ancestors) could not escape because Soviet troops moved into Hermannstadt (now Sibiu, about 41 miles from my village.)

As a reward for Romania's participation and cooperation during World War II, the Soviets gave most of Northern Transylvania back to Romania.

All citizens of Germanic descent were now considered "war criminals." The Romanians deported most of the young and middle-aged Saxon adults to the Soviet Union to make war reparations for damage inflicted by Nazi Germany. In January 1945, the first wave of them (30,000 of which were Transylvanian Saxon) were forcibly marched out of their villages, crammed into railroad cars, and hauled to Soviet labor camps. This event abruptly ended my childhood and ripped my family apart.

CHAPTER 2

Reichesdorf

R omania is a country in southeastern Europe, and is a little smaller than the state of Oregon. The village of Reichesdorf (now called *Richiş*) sits nestled at the foot of the Transylvanian Alps, right in the middle of Romania. It's beautiful with lush green hills, well-tended fertile fields, terraced vineyards, and in the distance, forest-covered mountains. During my childhood, most of the people in Reichesdorf made their living from farming, especially wine grapes.

About 1,000 German Saxons lived in Reichesdorf when I was growing up. We had no paved streets, no cars, no flush toilets, and no personal phones. (People in the bigger cities had these things, however.) We spoke Transylvanian Saxon (*Såksesch* – pronounced *"Sauxesh"*); worshiped as Lutherans; and valued faith, hard work, and education.

A few Romanians lived at the lower end of Reichesdorf. They had originally come to Reichesdorf to work for the Germans, and then stayed. These villagers spoke Romanian, had their own Orthodox Church, their own school, and painted their houses bright, awful colors. We Saxons kept our houses a subtle yellow or white. In the bigger cities, Romanians and Saxons may have mixed a little, but never in the small villages like Reichesdorf. A few Gypsies [people of Roma ethnicity] lived at the upper end of town. Some of them went to the Romanian school.

Reichesdorf Saxons always greeted one another on the streets because we all knew each other, like one big family. We had a town crier, who was also the post man, to spread important news throughout the village. He worked from the courthouse, which had the only phone in town.

Whenever a call came in about some big event or "breaking news," the postman would hurry through the village, beating his drum, and everyone would run out to hear the news. It was very exciting!

Reichesdorf, now called "*Richiș*"
The central, two-story building is the school.

The long building, center right, with cathedral windows, is the
community hall, and to its left, the courthouse.
The church sits behind the tall pines, with the bell tower to its right.
The homes have multiple buildings set up in squared "U" shapes,
with long courtyards down the center.

Reichesdorf had nine neighborhoods. My family lived in number four. These neighborhoods served to help each other out: to build houses, hold weddings, handle funerals, care for the sick, give support during disasters, and celebrate and care for newborns. This concept of community originated with our ancestors in Germany. A "Neighborhood Father" or "Church Father" headed each neighborhood. He would receive news or information from the minister or town officials then pass it on to everyone in his assigned neighborhood. The position rotated every two years. My father took his turns serving. The neighborhoods had their annual meeting every February. After taking care of business, we socialized with lots of visiting, singing, eating, and drinking.

Back in 1451, when the Reichesdorf Saxons built their church, they worshiped as Roman Catholics. During the Protestant Reformation in the 16th century, they followed their German motherland and converted to Lutheranism. As in the other villages, a high wall surrounded the church to protect the villagers from enemies. The Reichesdorf Saxons renovated the building in 1634 and again in 1895. They had to replace the roof two times: after a fire in 1600 and another one in 1702. In 1735 they rebuilt the loft, with a spiral staircase leading to it, and then built the altar 40 years later in 1775. The beautiful pipe organ is vintage 1788. Church members constructed the elevated pulpit in 1856, as well as the baptismal, which they made from stone and centered near the front of the church.

In 1890, when the villagers no longer needed a fortress wall around the church, they took most of the stones to build a new schoolhouse. They constructed it with two stories and a gym in the basement. The building held four classrooms and an apartment for the school superintendent.

During World War I, the Saxons melted down the church's tower bells for the war effort. After the war, they replaced them with the current bells (cast before that in 1908.)

In 1910, Reichesdorfers took the rest of the stones from the wall around the church to construct a community hall. They used it for celebrations, dances, school events, and plays. We had so many good times in that building!

CHAPTER 3

Coming into the World

For a more detailed description of my family tree and history, please see Chapter 12 at the end of the book.

Simon Untch, August 6, 1890 – October 8, 1949
Dressed here in his Austrian-Hungarian Navy uniform

Simon Untch (pronounced "Sĭ-mone Oŏnch")

My story begins with my father, *Simon Untch*. He was the third of eight children: *Johann, Adolf, Simon, Samuel, Friedrich, Wilhelm, Katharina,* and *Andreas.* When he was younger, his friends called him *"Fuchs"* ("fooks") – fox – because he had red hair. His older brothers teased him about his hair, so he would tattle to his father. Consequently, Johann and Adolf would receive spankings. Once, they got even with Simon by locking him in the barn.

At about 19 years old, Simon left to serve in the Austrian-Hungarian Navy for a four-year commission. WWI hit at the end of his duty, obligating him to serve for four more years. During this term, he kept watch for enemy ships in the Mediterranean Sea. While serving, he wrote an article about his experiences for a local magazine

German Farmer on a Voyage

At the beginning of the war, I was assigned to the "Prince Eugene." That is where I learned to operate the engine. We tested the coal-fired engine. We were stationed at the Port of Pola.

Then the order came. We were given notice to be on alert. There were two German ships in danger. "Goben" and "Breslau" were getting coal and provisions when they realized that the British and French were spying on them. German ships could only stay in port for 48 hours because Italy was not yet a part of the war. We fired up our engines and readied our ammunition and food supplies. We said our good-byes. There was a lot of smoke from the coal-fired engines in the air. The signal was given, "All men aboard." We began our journey. Submarines, torpedo ships, destroyers and all sailed slowly, one after the other, past the Admiral's ship, "Biribus

Unitius. The trumpet was blowing and the flagman was giving signals. This is how the important orders were issued. And so they went off to sea. The music of a hymn floated in the air. It was a beautiful day when we took to sea. I was fortunate to see the whole fleet from my vantage point on the upper deck. We were standing by with rescue boats. The maneuvers lead us to believe we were undefeatable. We sailed the entire day and part of the night through the Adriatic Sea. Then the order came to prepare for battle. I volunteered to load the 15-cm canon. Word came that the enemy torpedo boat was in sight. It was the dark of night and we couldn't see. A message came over the wireless from the "Goben" that luck was with them and they had gotten away from the British and French. They were sailing for Constantinople. I was disappointed. Not one shot. We were ready for battle and certain we would win. After we got to port, we drank and sang. When we took off again, we headed north.

After a year and a half I got leave from Pola and went home. My father had written and asked me to bring clothes for my four younger brothers. I packed the clothes into a backpack. A friend helped me carry the heavy backpack to the train station. After a happy goodbye, the train rolled for two and a half days through the hills to Graz. There I bought another bag full of gifts. I would have had to wait nine hours for a connecting train. Not being sleepy or patient, I shouldered the bags and walked the 26-KM to Reichesdorf. Like every time I make a decision, the time went fast. There was a half moon and I could see the way. My thoughts were already at home when I got to Mediasch. I thought about leaving the bag in Mediasch so it wouldn't slow me down. I knew everyone was waiting at home. Mediasch was deep in sleep. I told myself, "You are a soldier, you can carry 30 Kilo." I kept going. The night engulfed me. My thoughts were on my mother. I couldn't believe it was true that she had died a few months earlier.

Mother was gone. My sister had married and left home. How would I find everything? My mind was racing and I realized I had to stop and catch my breath. I heard the sound of the mill, and the miller's dog barking. I got up and started on my way again. The moon had gone down behind the hill, but I knew the way from childhood, when I used to go to town with my father. I would ask him, who does this field belong to? Whose orchard is this? Whose grapes are those? Whose pasture is this? Whose buildings are these? I asked him many things, until he was tired of answering. I could see the hill where I used to tend the cattle as a boy. This was where I shook from fright when the thunder and lightning brought rain and hail. I spent many hours here watching the cows. As I got closer to home, more and more memories came flooding back. I thought about how important the soil is to the farmer. It was as if the fields were greeting me. To a farmer, the land is almost sacred. That's what we fight for. The sun was starting to rise; I heard the rooster crow. People were stirring. Cows were mooing. Horses were neighing.

Every creature wanted to greet me.

As I got to our house, my father was opening the door. He was surprised to see me on foot so early in the morning. We greeted one another. All my brothers came and greeted me, too. Then we all went in the house, my father beside me. Everything was there, except my mother. She had died from too much work and too many cares.

By Simon Untch
(Translated by Anna Untch Melgaard.)

Family Troubles

Simon's mother, *Katharina Schuster Untch*, died of an illness when Simon was 23, six months into the war. There were still five children at home with Simon's father, *Johann Untch*: Samuel, Friedrich, Wilhelm, Katharina, and Andreas. Before she died, their mother had also taken in her sister's newborn baby, Sara, orphaned at childbirth. Simon's widowed father needed help with the children. Typhoid fever had left Samuel partially deaf in second grade and Friedrich completely deaf at the age of six. The youngest, Andreas, was only about eight years old when their mother died. Baby Sara eventually went to live with other relatives, and then on to an orphanage in Bierthalm.

There was a woman in Bierthalm whose husband was missing in action from the war. She moved into Johann's house and cooked, cleaned and cared for the children. She and Johann lived as if they were husband and wife. Johann's sons and even the minister talked to him and told him that what he was doing wasn't right. But, Johann couldn't marry the woman from Bierthalm; she wasn't technically a widow.

Rosina Greger
April 10, 1897 – August 5, 1981

Rosina Greger (pronounced "*Rozeena*")

My mother, *Rosina Greger*, was the oldest of five children: two sisters, *Regina* and *Anna*; and two brothers *Fredrich* and *Johann*. When times were tough in Romania and her Grandfather Geltch went to Australia to find work, Rosina lived with her Grandmother Geltch to help her out.

She was very ambitious and tireless, and finished 8 years of school in Reichesdorf, the highest grade in those days. By the time she turned 18, all the young men had gone off to war and she feared she'd be an old maid. But she needn't have worried; the young men who survived WWI returned before she turned 22.

In winter, it was customary for the girls to get together after dinner and do hand work. They took turns hosting, so the group went to a different house each night. Everyone talked and sang while they worked. On one of those evenings, Rosina was spinning yarn with the girls when a few young men came to visit. Simon Untch was among them. At the end of the evening, he noticed that Rosina had more spindles filled with yarn than any of the other girls. Then and there, he decided to court her.

Rosina Greger and Simon Untch Wedding picture 1919

Moving into the Family Home

Rosina and Simon married in 1919 and moved into the family home with his father, his siblings, and the woman from Bierthalm. A house usually passed to the first son, but Simon's oldest brother, Johann, had gone to live in America and his next oldest brother, Adolf, married a woman whose family had a house for them. So Simon would eventually inherit the home. Also back then, when people married, their families gave them enough to get started. Simon and Rosina received two cows and two pieces of land with which to begin their married life.

Rosina and Simon were soon pregnant with their first child. Not long after, the woman from Bierthalm became pregnant with Johann's child. This was a very big shame in those days because they weren't married.

Rosina gave birth to her first baby, Katharina, on January 25, 1920. Not long after, the woman from Bierthalm gave birth to Johann's little girl. While the woman was recovering, Rosina cooked the meals.

A Sad Homecoming

The woman's husband had survived the war after all, and returned to find his wife living with Johann Untch. On August 6, 1920, when Johann was bringing home a load of hay from Bierthalm, the woman's husband shot him. Then, he went to the other side of Reichesdorf and shot himself.

The woman and her little girl moved back to Bierthalm. From then on, the Untch family didn't have anything to do with Simon's half-sister and they *never* spoke of the incident. As a child, I visited my Grandmother Katharina's grave in the cemetery and wondered where my Grandfather Johann's grave was. It wasn't until we were adults that my cousin Katharina Untch Kloos [Uncle Dolf's daughter] told me the story. Grandfather hadn't been allowed to be buried in the cemetery because of having lived in sin.

Eventually, the only people living in the family home were Simon, Rosina, baby Katharina, and Simon's younger brother, Friedrich. Andreas left home while still a teenager and found his way to Vancouver, BC Canada. Katharina married but died of a stroke in her late 20s. Simon and Rosina inherited Friedrich ("Fritz") along with the house. Since he had become deaf at six years old, he didn't get any schooling. So, the responsibility to care for him fell to Mother. He would make noises, trying to talk, but we were never able to understand him. We used our own sign language to talk to him or call him to dinner. He had his own piece of land to work and was helpful in that respect. Even after Father died, Mother took care of Uncle Fritz until he passed away.

Simon and Rosina had three more children before I came into the world: a boy named Simon, a girl named Regina, and another boy. The boys did not survive infanthood, however. They had both been named "Simon." On September 13, 1926, I joined my older sisters, Katharina and Regina.

The Untch Family inside our courtyard, in front of the hay barn
(A tapestry is hung over the barn door for a backdrop)
Back row: Mother, Father, Kathi, and Mother's youngest sister,
Anna Front row: Yinni and me
(Another baby is hiding behind Yinni, inside Mother's stomach.)

Katharina (pronounced "*Kaught-a-reena*") nicknamed Kathi
("*Kaugh-ty*")

Kathi was six years older than me and pretty bossy. Of course, it was her job to take care of us younger kids when Mother and Father were out working. She got into trouble if anything went wrong. She was sick a lot growing up. After she finished school in Reichesdorf, she went to a special school in another town to learn advanced weaving. She grew interested in a guy she met there, but my Father came home one day and said she was not to have anything more to do with him. So that was the end of that. Because of the years between us, I would never have guessed that one day, she and I would become very close and, in turns, help to save each other's lives.

Regina (pronounced "*Rĕ-geena*" with a hard g) nicknamed Yinni
("*Jinnee*" with a slurred j)

Yinni was almost three years older than me. She had flat feet and had to have them operated on when she was almost a teenager. The operations weren't very successful, however, and her options in life were somewhat limited. After finishing school, she wanted to get out on her own, go places, and see things. But, because of her feet, she ended up staying at home.

Me, Anna (pronounced "*Aha-na*")

Johann (pronounced "*Yohaan*") nicknamed Hans

Hans came along four years after me. Father finally had a boy that lived! They decided not to name him Simon. When Hans arrived, I had to give up my baby bed – a dresser drawer in our parents' room. I moved into the kid's room, into a big bed with my two older sisters. They put me in the middle so I wouldn't fall out. I remember my parents calling, "Go to sleep in there!" so we must have had a good time, talking and giggling.

Rosina (pronounced "*Rozeena*") nicknamed Sinni ("*Zinnee*")

Sinni joined the family, seven years after Johann, ten and a half years after me. When the time came, Father sent my sister Kathi for the midwife while he boiled water. The midwife made it to our house in time. I never heard Mother scream. (Boy! I sure screamed when it was my turn!) Not long after, Father cried, "Another girl!" He'd wanted another boy, but he was proud of us girls, too. They put two chairs together near the stove and laid some blankets on them to keep the baby warm. Mother knew I wanted to see the baby and said it was okay to go look at her.

We did most things together as a family, whether we were working in the fields, going to church, getting together with cousins, celebrating holidays, etc. Family is the most important thing. I wish everyone would know how important family is. It is heartbreaking when people from the same family don't talk to each other. They are missing out on so much. Please remember to forgive. Pride is a foolish thing.

The following photo was buried in a barrel. But water seeped in and ruined spots of this photograph and others.

My Family later, outside our home
Back row: Yinni, me, and Kathi
Front row: Mother, Hans, and Father, and between them, little Sinni

CHAPTER 4

Growing Up on the Family Farm, the Good Life

O ur family worked hard. Even the little children had jobs and learned the value of hard work early in life. We farmed and grew or made nearly everything we needed. Father was a good business man as well, growing grapes and making and selling wine and grappa (*poli* in Såksesch, a type of grape pomace brandy or clear liqueur.) He continually bought more plots of land and increased our production.

My parents often hired as many as ten people a day to help with the fieldwork: hoeing, planting, securing grape posts, tying grapes, spraying, and harvesting. We did everything manually. The field hands slept in our hay loft and Mother cooked for them. She also had a maid to help with us kids. The maid was married to Father's year-round, hired hand.

We grew fruit trees, grain, potatoes, corn, beets, and more on our flat land. Grapevines lined our sloping acres. And forests covered the steep hills. We didn't need to irrigate; it rained enough to do the job. And boy, it could really rain! Romania was lush and beautiful.

Since everyone lived in the village, miles away from their crops, the farmers built shacks in their fields so the workers could have shelter during a hard rain or hail. We had many rain shacks (*kalips* in Såksesch) for our many fields. Even the animals had shelters out there. At least one of our field shacks was large enough to hold our family and Father's work crew. It had a table with benches, a loft that folded out over the table, a stove, and a few provisions. Mother would serve us and the workers lunch there. My sister, Katharina, thought it would be fun to spend the night in the loft, but our parents said "No." I thought it would be too scary, so far away from home.

Winter covered everything in a thick layer of white. Father had to shovel paths through the snow around our courtyard. He would dump the snow in the river, near our street. We didn't go into the fields during those months. The men, however, would go into the forests to get firewood.

Chores

Some of my childhood chores were to carry in wood and set the table. In the summer, I hauled water to the workers. It was a lot of work and when I got tired, I sat down. Next thing I knew, someone would call, "Anna, we're thirsty!"

While the adults worked in the fields, my brother Hans and I watched the cattle. We used whips to herd them. I remember more than once we got so involved in playing that, when we finally looked up, all the cows were gone! We found them in the vineyard. This was very bad. To keep from getting into trouble, we drug a tree branch along the ground to cover up the hoof prints.

Hoof prints can be very incriminating.

The kids also prepared the grapevines for grafting. My sisters and I took some grape root stalk and cut it so it had two eyes left. Then, we cut up a vine from the good, fungus-free plants so there would be one eye on each piece. Next, we placed the cut vines in moss and sawdust and put them in the summer kitchen to stay warm. We had to keep them moist throughout the winter. In spring, when the plants were ready, the men did the grafting.

In the evenings, my family would come in from the fields together and get right to work on our chores. Mother would fix dinner and Father would work on projects around the house. The boys did their boy chores and the girls their girl chores: feeding animals, collecting eggs, milking cows, cleaning the house, setting the table . . . . And boy, we had better get our chores done!

Father was very strict with us when we were old enough to know the rules. He believed if kids had too much time on their hands, they would only get into trouble. If we played for too long, or played when we were supposed to be working, (which happened often) he would tell us to go pick a switch for him to spank our bottoms with. It was so hard to decide which branch would be best. Was it better to get a thicker or a thinner branch? Which one would sting more?

Sometimes, after a spanking, I went to mother for comfort. She would explain why Father had punished me and how I could do better the next time.

Father was very serious and expected a lot from us, but I loved him very much.

As I grew, I became quite the housekeeper. Once, I found some dirt on the threshold that the maid had missed. I swept it up and was so proud! Also, it used to bother me that the cows would have to use their own stall for a bathroom. I would remove the cow pies so they could have a clean stall. Mother would ask me, "Don't you have enough to do in the house?"

My Mother

My mother was a good mother – the best: patient and kind and very hard working. If we got too loud, she would say, "You're just like the Gypsies!" They could often be heard yelling from their hill outside of town. I can remember once when she stood over me, shaking her fist. But she never laid a hand on us. When I was too tired to do the dishes, she stayed up and finished them. It always amazed me how tirelessly she worked. She would get up in the middle of the night to start making bread for the hired hands. The workers always received sandwiches from her at lunchtime. Many days, she would labor very hard in the fields alongside the other workers. Even when resting, she would sew, spin yarn, weave, knit, crochet, embroider, or make other handcrafts.

My Father

Father liked to read the newspaper, which was delivered to Reichesdorf. I remember him wearing his glasses and if you asked him a question, he would look at you over the top of them. He was interested in politics. I remember him making arrangements for political speakers to come talk to the community. He also gave classes on grafting grapes. Wild roses grew everywhere around our village and Father enjoyed experimenting with them. He would graft wild roses to cultivated ones. Consequently, we had a variety of roses around our home. When he served his turn as Neighborhood Father, he faithfully saw to the well-being of our neighborhood and passed communications from Rev. Herberth to all the families.

People would ask Father what to do when they had a sick loved one. He advocated the "water cure," using a book from his mother that he referenced. When one of us came down with a fever, he would have us sit in a tub of cold water. Then, we would hop out, wrap our self in blankets until we warmed up, and then get back into the cold tub. In winter, he would send us running barefoot in the snow, back and forth across the yard. Then, we would run inside, put on our socks, and get really warm. This was supposed to be good for circulation. For colds and earaches, he would set us up with a steam bath, where we'd lean over a tub of hot water with a towel over our head. He also made a special poultice recipe for boils.

House #118 in Neighborhood 4

We lived close enough to the center of Reichesdorf that I could see the bell tower and its clock from my bedroom window. Each morning, I would wake up and see it first thing. Several generations of the Untch family were born and grew up in our big house. Like many other houses in Reichesdorf, it included a conglomeration of structures fronted by a high wall running alongside the street. The wall had a large gate in the middle of it for animals and farm implements, (wagons, plows, disks . . . .) and a smaller door to the right for people. Both entries led into the courtyard, which was surrounded by buildings. Our house was on the right of the courtyard, a summer kitchen on the left, various sheds and barns beyond those, and a well pump in the middle.

The house, made of brick covered by stucco, had a basement, a main floor, and an attic. The main floor included a front room, a large kitchen, and two, large bedrooms. One of our relatives liked to paint and every so often he'd paint the plaster walls a different color. He also used stencils to paint a border of flowers or other designs around the top of the walls in the kitchen and living room.

Our kitchen was a very large living area, somewhat like an American great room. We cooked on, and heated the house with, a wood burning stove. Its chimney pipe passed through other rooms before venting to the outside. The family ate together around a long table. Grapes hung around the edges of the ceiling, turning into raisins in the heat from the stove. After dinner during the cold months, we sat in this room and worked on our sewing and weaving projects. Uncle Fritz slept there, in a fold-out bed. As children, we thought it would be very exciting to sleep in that bed, in the kitchen. The benches around the table could also open up into beds for guests. Every bit of space was useful and every piece of furniture built to last.

Parents and small children slept in one of the bedrooms, with the baby in a large dresser drawer. Older children slept in another room. Our beds included sack-mattresses stuffed with straw, and bedding filled with feathers. They folded up against the wall, like Murphy beds, so the rooms could be used for visiting.

We called the front room, on the street-side of the house, "the cold room" because it didn't have a stove. Mother and Father stored a lot of our food in there.

To get up into the attic, we climbed a sturdy ladder in the kitchen. It had wide footing for hauling up heavy loads. There we kept nuts, beans, onions, corn, and other grains. Our dormant bees slept up there through the winter. And, when it rained, Mother dried our clothes up there.

In the cellar, we stored vegetables as well as our barrels of wine. You could access it from inside the house by wooden steps, or from outside by a ramp for rolling the wine barrels in and out.

Sheds and Barns

Up the yard, right next to our house, a shed held a large wagon, two grape presses, and stacks of firewood. Beyond the shed, a cement floor and brick walls housed our pigs. Further up the yard sat a cow barn, and across the top of the yard a hay barn. Our outhouse stood at the upper end of the yard, too. It smelled pretty bad, but you got used to it. Next, down the other side of the yard, was the manure pile, and then another barn for two small wagons and more wood storage.

The Summer Kitchen

The last building, bordering the street and directly across the court-yard from our house, sat a two-room, summer kitchen (used in the hot months to keep the heat away from the house.) One of the rooms had a big, brick oven for baking bread and drying fruit, a wood stove for cooking, and a long, long table with benches on either side. Here, Mother fed the family and hired hands. Also, the room had a tub up on legs for washing dishes and laundry. The other room in the summer kitchen housed two, pulp-stomping pits and a still.

In the middle of the courtyard stood our well pump, which we pumped by hand to draw water. We pumped and pumped … always pumping. We pumped for drinking and cooking, and for making pig slop (boiled potatoes and other vegetables stomped into mush.) The Fire Department required every house to keep an uncovered barrel full of water by the pump, the size of a wine barrel. We kids would often play in it during the summer, splashing around until half the water was gone. We would get into so much trouble! Oh, but it was *such* fun. How could we resist?

Electricity

During my youngest years, we lit our house with oil lamps: glass lamps with rope wicks. Father and Mother didn't allow me to touch them.

Sometime in the 1930s, when I was about eight, we got elec-tricity. It was very exciting! Men came to the house, working all over the place: pounding, spreading wires, and saying things like,

"Turn it on over there. Now, turn it on over here." When we turned the new lights on, the rooms were so bright! We continued to use the wood stoves for cooking and heat, however.

Mother had always used a pedal sewing machine. When we got electricity, Father brought her home an electric one. It had a pedal shaped like a foot. Mother used it to wind spools of thread as well as to sew. The wiring from the machine to the wall wasn't quite right, so once in a while, she would get a shock and holler out. It always surprised us to hear her yell, as she was normally such a quiet woman.

Gas didn't come to Reichesdorf until 1958, a long time after I'd gone.

Land

My family had many parcels of land outside of Reichesdorf. Father was always saving money to buy more. He would buy land over household goods, like new mattresses. This was smart, though. If a hailstorm destroyed the crop in one field, the other fields would be fine, we wouldn't lose everything.

Most of the land was too steep for large machinery, like tractors, so a lot of the work had to be done by hand. Our biggest farm implements included: a large wagon for hay and grape harvests, two small wagons for daily use, a plow that would tip over to do the next pass, and a harrow. We had two grape presses: an old, large, square one; and a newer, small, round one. Farmers could also rent machinery from a co-op in Reichesdorf.

Our primary income came from grapes. For ourselves, we raised apples, cherries, peaches, nectarines, apricots, prunes, nuts, potatoes, wheat, and lots and lots of corn. Romania was king of all corn! We took our wheat or corn to the mill to be ground, and then brought it home to bake bread in our large, summer kitchen oven.

We also raised bees for honey and wax. For the animals, we grew beets, alfalfa, oats, and barley. If we harvested more than we needed, we sold it.

Animals

We didn't have any pets, really, only farm animals. Each family had a few kinds: chickens, pigs, cows, oxen, domestic water buffalo, and/or horses. Farmers used cows, oxen, buffalo, or horses to pull their wagons to the fields. Father, however, had no use for horses. He said they tended to run away and would knock everything down in their path. He also hated dogs because one stole his lunch once. We had lots of cats, though, to catch mice. And, there were chickens – all over – that made us hunt for their eggs. We'd find one here, one there …. Sometimes we'd come upon a huge, hidden pile. To see if they were good or bad, we'd put them in water. If they sank, they were good; if they floated, they were bad.

Father preferred cows to oxen or buffalo because they were the most useful. He usually had at least four of them to wear the yolks for the big wagon. They bore calves, which enabled us to butcher a cow now and then. And, when not worked too hard, they supplied us with milk.

Buffalo (*Büffel)* were stronger than cows, but produced mostly cream and not as much milk.

We had two brood sows in the stall at the upper end of the yard. I spent a lot of time watching the piglets play. They were so cute!

Rabbits and other wild animals lived in the fields and forests, but we didn't trap or hunt any. The government didn't allow us to have guns. One man must have had a license to hunt wild pigs, however. We would see him walking through town with all his hunting dogs.

Grapes

As soon as the snow melted, usually in March, our family and hired hands walked or rode in the wagons several miles out to the vineyards. We kids watched the cows while the grown-ups pruned grapevines. Then, my brother and sisters and I took pitchforks and pushed the clippings to the end of the row, beside the road. When the clippings dried, we came back and burned them.

Lunch Break in the Vineyard
With relatives and friends from Schlatt
I enjoyed working together with the family.
Kathi is in the back with arm out Mother is in the middle front with white scarf
I am to the right of mother with white apron, little Sinni next
to me Yinni is behind Sinni

You can see the grape plants behind us in the photo. The center posts are clearly seen above the grape plants. Later we would train the vines to loop to the center post, making a heart shaped form so the sun could reach all the grapes.

In the next picture there are three heads together on the left side of the back row. I am the one in the middle. Yinni is in the back row standing on the wagon, white scarf and blouse. Kathi is sitting on the tongue of the wagon on the left all dark clothing. Sinni is sitting above the left front wagon wheel.

The men hauled in the new, locust wood posts they had prepared during the winter and replaced any old posts that were too worn. Then, the women tied up to four vines to each post, looping the branches up, out, and down, making heart shapes. We tied the vines with soaked, pliable hemp. After that, we spaded the soil.

Two or three times during the growing season, we came back to the vineyard to hoe up the weeds and do the green work - tying up all the green shoots- so that the sun could shine through to the grapes and so the men could spray.

Unfortunately, *peronospora,* a fungus known as "downy mildew," thrived in our abundant moisture. You couldn't see it, but it caused the leaves to burn and dry up. It affected the grapes as well; they, too, would dry up and fall off. In my grandparents' time, this fungus ruined all the vineyards and caused an economic depression. Mother's father, Grandfather Greger had to leave Romania to find work. (Fortunately, he got job in America as a tailor and was able to send money back to his family.) Once the farmers learned to graft disease-free grapes, agriculture was profitable enough that he could return to Romania.

To prevent downy mildew, the grapevines had to be sprayed at least four times a year with sulfur. To make the spray, we purchased lime and fungicide and mixed them with water. Father and his hands loaded a big water tank onto the wagon and drove it to the vineyard. We filled buckets with water, from a spigot on the big tank, and poured it into spray tanks that contained the lime and fungicide. Men carried the spray tanks on their backs, walking down one row and back up the next, coating the vines with a bluish hue from the spray.

Grape harvest usually started in October. Father yoked the cows to pull our largest wagon, loaded with a big, open barrel, into the vineyard. With knives or clippers, we picked the grapes into buckets. When our buckets were full, we dumped the grapes into a wooden "*bot*," a barrel with shoulder straps. It had a flat side to go against a man's back. A hired man would mash the grapes into the *bot* with a pronged stick so we could get more in. When it was full, he hefted it onto his back and climbed up onto the wagon. By tilting his body just so – a skill that took practice – the grapes and juice would slide into the big barrel. When the big barrel was full, we got to go home.

Mother would have whisky and bread waiting for us, which were supposed to prevent stomach problems from eating too many grapes. The men drank a shot of whisky and the children had a couple of drops on a sugar cube. Then, we all ate slices of bread.

Time to press the grapes! We unloaded our harvest into the presses, which Father or the hired man would tighten several times, until late at night. The juice ran through a trough to the cellar and into barrels. The next morning, Father would tighten them again.

Workers scooped out the left-over pulp from the presses and hauled it across the yard into one of the cement pits in the summer kitchen. Two children had to stomp on the mostly dry pulp to pack it down and expel the air. Sometimes, an ornery hired hand would dump more pulp in on top of us. We made sure to run into the corners when the next load arrived! When the pit was full, Father or the hired man covered the pit tightly to keep the air out.

Every day, including Sundays, we repeated the whole process.

Once the pulp ("pomace") fermented, Father shoveled it into the still to make grappa, (we called it "poli") a type of pomace brandy or clear liqueur. Reichesdorf also had two community stills for those who didn't have their own. After the distilling process, the hired hands threw the remaining pulp onto the fields for fertilizer.

During the wine fermenting process, Father tended the juice. No one else was allowed in the cellar because the fumes were too strong. From time to time, he would siphon it from one barrel to another. He also distilled the sediment leftover from the siphoning. Nothing was wasted.

I loved the smells of our Reichesdorf farm: the abundant produce, Father's roses, breads baking, and Mother's Sunday roast beef and homemade gravy. However, I did *not* like the wine-making smells. The fermentation process really stank!

When the wine was ready, people came from all over to purchase it. Father, a good businessman, bought wine from other farmers as well, and sold it later for a better price. One buyer, who I think had a pool hall, would drive over from Hungary and load his truck with Father's barrels. He really knew how to stay in our good graces: he brought us children chocolate bars!

Corn Harvest

We inter-planted corn with pole beans. Once the seedpods of the red and white beans dried, we harvested them first. After grape harvest, we picked the corn by hand and brought the ears to the house kitchen to husk. The husks went in one pile and the ears in another. People came over to help, making the work light and fun. For laughs, a girl would lie on the floor while the others stuffed cornhusks in her skirt. When they helped her up, her skirt looked like a balloon. The husks were pretty itchy and everyone giggled as she danced around like a scarecrow to get them out. Afterward, we took the husks out for the cows to eat and the ears up to the attic to dry.

During the winter, Father and my uncles used dried corn husks to make entryway mats for scraping dirt off our shoes. They twisted or tied the husks together in such a way that the tougher, thickest ends were sticking straight up.

When the ears of corn dried, we ran them through a machine with a crank. The cob came out in one place, and the kernels in another. Cobs made good fire-starters for the stove. We stored the kernels until we needed them, and then only had a small amount ground at a time, especially in summer. If we left ground corn in the bin too long, the oil in the flour would turn it stale and lumpy.

Father cut down the corn stalks later, when he had time. We'd prop them up in a teepee shape to dry, then chop them into foot-long pieces and feed them to the cows.

Grain

Each farmer raised as much corn, flour, oats, and barley as his family and animals needed. Reichesdorf had two grist mills. The oldest one, just outside the village, was driven by water. I remember seeing its huge wheel in the stream when Father took me with him to have some grain ground. A newer mill, inside the village, used electricity.

Food Preserving

The women canned cherries, currants and tomatoes. They put the produce in jars with sugar water and covered the jars with a special kind of heavy wax paper. With a small amount of water in a kettle, they boiled the produce in the jars. The wax would melt and seal the jars. Then, they stored the jars in the cold room at the front of the house. Our family made jams, but not a lot as sugar was hard to come by. Sometimes, if there was no jam, we ate bread with honey and butter.

My parents put up wire around the edges of the ceiling of the cold room. This we used to hang bacon, as well as grapes, tying the clusters onto the wires with string. Along the wooden floor, we lined boxes of apples and pears. These fruits kept through most of the winter.

We made our cabbage into sauerkraut by cutting the core out of each head, pouring salt into the holes, dumping the cabbages into an open barrel – one layer on top of another – then filling the barrel with water to submerge the heads. Every time someone went down into the cellar, they had to brush the top of the water with a large branch of thyme to keep skim and foam from forming on top. After a month or two, when we wanted to have cabbage, we pulled out a head and chopped it up for dinner.

Mother also kept carrots and parsnips in the cellar, buried in sand.

Butchering a Pig

Twice each winter, Father and his brother, Uncle Dolf, butchered a pig. One of them killed the pig by sticking a knife straight into its neck. The blood would shoot out and the other man would catch it in a pan to use for blood sausage. Then, they put a little straw around the pig and lit a match to singe off all its hair. After that, Father and Uncle Dolf scrubbed the skin clean and cut the pig open to pull out its parts. Mother took the liver inside to fry with onions and serve for dinner. This would be the first meal from the pig. She would also clean its intestines, turn them inside out, scrape them, and then soak them – a process repeated several times – so they could be used for sausage casings.

As a child, I stuck my nose into everything, eager to see and to know. The butchering process especially fascinated me and I watched intently. Once, Uncle Dolf, a great teaser, cut off the pig's tail and chased after me. It scared me and I ran and hid behind the door. As he often did, he laughed his big, hearty laugh. Uncle Dolf was quite a character. You could always tell when he was around because of his wonderful laugh.

When it came time to grind the meat, I would watch it come out of the grinder and wonder what was inside the machine. One time, when Kathi was doing the grinding, I stuck my finger in and found out. That's why the knuckle of my right index finger is crooked.

We seasoned and mixed the ground meat with other meats or grains, stuffed it into the intestine casings, and then took some to all the relatives. Our family made three kinds of sausages: red sausage, white sausage (*weisswurst* – made with more veal than pork,) and blood sausage (*blutwurst* – made with blood.) If each family staggered their butchering and shared with the rest, we all had a continual supply of fresh sausage.

Mother rendered [melted and strained] the lard, and roasted the meat. In order to preserve the meat, she poured the lard over it. In a cold place, the meat could last many months encased in the congealed fat. During the winter, she hung meat in the attic. This we would eat soon. For the bacon, she left the rind [the skin] on, and we laid it out in the summer kitchen to salt it.

Sometimes, we smoked it. Then, we hung it up in the cold room.

Bees

In springtime, Father took our bees out to the fields, close to the orchards and grapes. We probably had a couple dozen beehives. I remember him getting into a funny outfit, which included a big hat with a net to cover his face and neck. He pumped smoke at the hives through a big pipe to calm the bees and so they wouldn't sting.

In the fall, Father pulled honeycombs out of the hives and put them in a machine that would extract the honey. The children turned the machine's handle slowly, but inside, the combs spun very fast and the honey flew onto the sides of the machine. The honey would drip down the sides and out of the bottom of the machine into an enamel or glass bowl. Some years, we had so much honey Mother didn't know where to put it all! In winter, Father moved the hives back into our attic. One year, something happened and almost all of the bees died.

Soap

We made our own soap with three kilos of tallow, one kilo of lye, and five liters of water. My parents purchased the tallow from the butcher shop. Mother boiled the ingredients in a large pot, stirring the mixture with a wooden paddle. Since it had to be stirred continuously, I often got to help. It took a long time for the tallow to melt and for the soap to gather on the stick. Once the soap cooled, hardened and dried, we cut it into pieces. Mother used the leftover water to wash clothes and clean floors.

Hemp

My family also raised hemp. From it we made cord, yarn, and thread. Growing quality hemp required good soil and carefully prepared ground. After plowing and disking the soil, Father ran a spike tooth or harrow (pulled by the cows) over it. In late May, he cast the seeds by hand. If he sowed them too closely, the plants would be stunted; if too sparsely, the hemp would grow branches and be too coarse. Some people thought hemp had to be planted during a certain phase of the moon for it to grow right. I didn't believe this. The way to grow perfect hemp is a mystery. It takes a little feeling in the fingers when sowing the seeds, good luck, and a blessing from above for everything to come together.

The plants would grow to four or five feet tall, usually by early August, and ready for harvest. First, we pulled each one out of the ground and shook the dirt off the roots. Then, the adults bundled the stocks and the children tied each bundle with two, short pieces of hemp cord. To help the hemp dry faster, we stood the bundles on end in groups of three, and propped them against each other like teepees, tied together at the top. After they dried, we knocked the leaves and seed heads off, usually by hitting the bundles against a bench. This work had to be done in dry, sunny weather. I loved to whack the hemp! We then tied and stacked the clean bundles in groups of ten, every other batch with the roots on the outside.

Next, the adults dammed the stream and laid the hemp in the water, tied to some posts so they would stay submerged. After two weeks of soaking, the yellowish outer layer of each stalk would be rotted and we could wash the bundles. The adults stood knee-deep in the stream (taking care not to be too close to the next person!) and slapped the bundles one at a time against the water until the outer layers were completely gone. Then, they tossed the bundles onto the creek bank and the children again stood them on end in teepee formation. Once completely dry, we all stacked the bundles in the wagon and took them home.

Back in our courtyard, adults used a special tool for breaking the woody middle layer of the hemp stalks into pieces. Then, we would swing the stalks against a pole or tree, causing the woody layer to splinter off. It took a finer tool to break the remaining woody layer apart. Again, we would beat the stalks against the pole until only little splinters of the woody layer were left. My family had a big iron comb that we dragged the stalks across until the last of the woody layer tore off, leaving only long, soft, stringy fibers. Mother stored these fibers for our winter weaving projects, and used the woody splinters for kindling.

**Bundling Hemp Fibers on the Sunny Side
of the Courtyard**

The older woman in the foreground is sister to my Aunt Anna in America. The woman is also an Untch but not directly related. (It was a small village; many had the same last names!) Her niece is on the far right - laughing. The rest are neighbors and friends.

The women tied the cleaned hemp fibers to a distaff, a 6-foot tall post. They pulled the fibers out with a spindle and twisted them to make thread. The more fibers pulled out, the thicker the thread would be. Children helped fill the spools. (There was always work for children to do!) Sometimes Mother dyed the hemp for weaving into patterns.

Aunt Anna's Sister Spinning Hemp

During bad weather, when we couldn't work outside, Mother wound the thread onto a warping board for weaving. It took a lot of thread, sometimes up to ten spools. She wound it around and around (sometimes 50 times) until it was the length of the cloth to be woven. Mother or Katharina tied the thread together in bunches of ten so it would be easier to move them to the loom. (Father had purchased the loom, but most of the other tools he'd made himself.) The thread had to be put onto the loom very carefully. Each and every one had to be threaded through a heddle eye. Finally, the hemp was ready to make into cloth!

On February 2nd, Maria Lichtmess Day, (the traditional Catholic Candlemass Day, or in America: Groundhog Day) the customary day to start weaving, women started their projects early in the morning. The beater bar of our loom made a certain, rhythmic sound, almost like music. When finished, Mother put the woven cloth in a tub, poured hot ash water over it, rinsed it, and hung it to dry. She took the cloth through this washing and drying process over and over, bleaching and softening the material. Children helped with the smaller pieces of cloth.

Out of the courser hemp, Mother wove floor mats. With the finer hemp, she wove tablecloths, towels, sheets, and clothing. She used the very finest threads to make underwear, which scratched at first until washed a few times. After Kathi returned from the advanced weaving school, where she'd made a really nice tablecloth, we wove a lot of different things.

Taking hemp from seed to cloth entailed a *lot* of work! But, the Saxons in Reichesdorf accomplished this feat because they were proud, ambitious, and hardworking people. Sadly, when the Soviet collective came along, the Saxons stopped planting hemp. Now, only the older ones among us know what it took to grow hemp and make cloth from it. I look now at the pieces I saved and remember with amazement all the effort that went into making them. And, as strong as hemp is, the cloth is still useful today.

Handcrafts

During the long, dark winters we rested from all our farm work. Of course, the women's hands still kept busy. Besides weaving, Mother and my sisters also knitted, crocheted, sewed, embroidered, and spun yarn.

Since we learned handcrafting in school, girls of different ages had different tasks. Even the little children had jobs, like filling the spools. As a young girl first learning to knit, I couldn't get the hang of the pearl stitch, and the yarn kept slipping off the end. I cried my heart out with frustration. Mother said, "Why would you cry about something like that?"

Meals

For breakfast, we usually had soup and bread. Some people had *Mămăligă* (cornmeal boiled in water, salted, and sometimes sweetened with a little sugar.) Father liked to have this for his supper. Maybe this was so Mother wouldn't have to cook after a hard day's work in the field.

At noon, we packed a picnic lunch for all the workers in the field. Mother included bacon and onion sandwiches, prune compote, and *Klabbert*, a yogurt-like food made with sour milk. For Saturday suppers, when we didn't have beef from one of our own cows, Mother sent me to the butcher shop to purchase some. She also used the beef to make a dumpling or noodle soup for Sunday's dinner. For desert, she'd bake some sort of treat, such as *Hunklich*: a flat, thin bread like a pizza, topped with eggs, cream, and sugar. It was so tasty! Dessert was my favorite.

Our farm always had fruit. It was our candy. We kids ran from relative to relative, to whoever had the best cherries, peaches, nectarines, and so forth. That's one thing I really miss about Romania: the fruit.

We milked our own cows, boiling the milk to pasteurize it so we wouldn't get sick. Sometimes, there would be an extra pail or two of milk to sell. Mother separated some of the cream to make butter and gave the skim milk to the pigs. Once in a while, we took milk to the village cheesemaker.

Clothing

Girls and women in Reichesdorf always wore dresses, never pants. Our socks covered our legs to above the knees, reaching the hem of our thigh-length underwear. We wore boots that laced up to just above the ankles.

Mother made our clothing from woven cotton, wool, or hemp. Sometimes, she bought the material and other times she wove it herself. We embroidered beautiful designs on the special outfits.

To do laundry, we put the dirty clothes or linens in a wine barrel tub that stood on legs, poured lye soap on top, and then poured hot water over all. It would bubble up. Then, we spread the wet clothes out on a bench and beat them with a paddle to work in the lye and soften the fabric. Next, we dipped the clothes in clean water to rinse, then laid them out and beat them again. To dry the clothes, we hung them up on lines across the yard.

Graduation Ceremony
My niece Regina is on the far left.
When students graduated, they were also confirmed in the church

A Wrist Watch

I was twelve or thirteen when people started wearing wristwatches, and I wanted one, too. Father told me I would appreciate a watch more if I earned it. So, he helped me get a job cleaning an office. I made the fire, swept the floor, and dusted the desk and furniture. The office needed to be warm by 8:00 am. It wasn't far to walk, but I had to get up earlier than usual. I worked there just until I had enough money for the watch.

Uncle Fritz Greger and his horses Otto and Bator took me to a jewelry store in Mediasch, where I found the watch I wanted and bought it. I was *so* proud of it, almost as if it were alive, as if I wasn't alone anymore! Watches were still quite a novelty at that time and, when I got home, everyone noticed my shiny new watch and commented on how nice it was. It meant a lot to me and I always wore it. I never even dreamed that someday I would have to sell it for food.

Family Fun

Grandparents

My Untch grandparents died before I came along. But, my Greger grandparents were alive and very much a part of our lives. **Rosina (Geltch) Greger**, Mother's mother, had been a Kindergarten teacher. She was fun to be with and very special to me.

We didn't have books when we were little, so Grandmother would come to our house and tell us stories like *Little Red Riding Hood* and *Hansel and Gretel*. As soon as I was big enough, I went to her house on Sundays. Some of the cousins came as well and we played out in the street, in the courtyard, or inside. We played hop-scotch and lots of different games with a ball. When they had time, my aunts would come too. They used these visits to catch up on news, since we had no phones.

Mother's father, **Andreas Greger**, usually just smoked his pipe and listened to all the chatter and play around him. I used to play with all the buttons he had brought back with him from America, when he'd gone there to work as a tailor.

Grandmother stopped keeping cows when she got older, so I took our extra milk to her. She always wanted to know who had done the milking. I think she liked the milk more if Father had done it, rather than the hired hand!

At about eleven or twelve years old, I went to help Grandmother out when she got sick. I tried to do a good job, kneading the bread very hard with my fists. She encouraged me, telling me what a good job I was doing. The next day, my knuckles were all red and sore.

I started taking my little brother with me to visit Grandmother. She would give us sugar cubes for our walks home. One day, when he was about six years old, Hans didn't want to go with me. I asked him why and he said that she smooched too much. He did *not* want to be kissed anymore!

Whenever the bells rang – morning, noon, and night – Grandmother would say, "God bless us."

My Father's brothers and their families gathered for a photo in front of our house #118. My Mother had purchased a bolt of material so each of the girl cousins would be able to wear the same shirts for the picture. Don't we all look like we belong together?

The Untch Families In front of our house, #118
Father and three of his brothers with their respective wives
and children below them:
Sitting left: Uncle Fritz

Standing left: Uncle Samuel, Aunt Sara below him holding
Johann, Johanna in front of Uncle Fritz, and Samuel Jr. bottom left.

My family is center: Father, Mother holding Hans, Kathi, me left
of her, and Yinni below me.

Top right: Uncle Dolf, Aunt Johanna, Johanna Jr. below her, Adolf
Jr. kneeling farthest right, Martin bottom right, and Katharina left
of him.

Cousins

Obviously, I had lots of cousins to play with. Playtime was Sunday
afternoon in the church yard. The worst punishment *ever* was to have
my Sunday afternoons taken away from me! We played hopscotch,
jacks, ball games, stick games, jump-rope games, and a game called
"Drop the Handkerchief."

We bounced little rubber balls against walls, trying to see how
many times we could hit a wall before the ball fell to the ground,

or how many times we could turn around after a throw before it bounced back and we caught it. Kids said rhymes with the games, like *Tipi Tapi*. We crocheted holders to wear around our necks so our little balls wouldn't get lost.

My cousins and friends and I enjoyed a game similar to baseball. We used a leather ball stuffed with horsehair, which didn't bounce like our rubber balls. And we had *Klepsch:* a wood batting game where we'd knock a pointed piece of wood (1" wide and 4" long) with a board (4" x 13") up in the air, then hit it as far as possible. If the other team caught it, they were up. It was a lot like Fly Up, only with wood instead of a ball. We also played a game like hopscotch with a piece of roof tile.

In the winter, we skied, sledded, and ice skated. During bad weather that kept us inside for long, boring hours, the girls played jacks with little bones from a pig, or our favorite: Mill – *Mühle*.

For Mill, someone drew three squares on a piece of paper, one inside the other. Each player took turns putting their pieces (corn kernels, pebbles, nuts, or beans) on the corners and lines until the pieces were lined up and they could bump the other player off of a square.

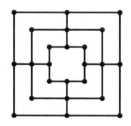

Game Board for *Mühle*

We sang and danced all the time, just for fun or in more organized ways. Our teachers taught us songs in kindergarten, such as the meal blessing, "Kom Herr Jesus (come Lord Jesus) . . ." We learned nursery rhymes, church songs, and silly songs. The older kids might have sung love songs.

Dance lessons started at home, in our big kitchen-family room. Father taught us, mostly. The steps sometimes involved moving in place, and other times swinging around. We'd laugh and laugh at ourselves and each other when we messed up.

At school dances in the community hall, the teachers chose the songs and taught the dancing. The younger girls never danced with boys. We hated to dance with boys! The adults and youth danced in groups and in pairs, depending on the dance.

Village Life

Church

Our highly educated Saxon minister, Andreas Herberth, was an important leader of the village during all of my years in Romania. He explained our laws and settled conflicts. (I always thought Father made all the rules, until I read *Reichesdorf*, edited by Andreas Nemenz, and found that the minister had compiled them!) He established community practices and procedures, and studied the almanac before sending written notes around when it was time to plant or spray.

Rev. Herberth preached from the high pulpit when leading church services. He sang with his back to the congregation, facing Jesus on the cross, and the congregation sang the responses. (He couldn't sing very well, but it was what it was.) Families sat separately during the services: men on the sides of the sanctuary, boys in the loft, women in the middle and toward the back, and girls up front facing the adults on the opposite side of the pulpit and baptismal.

Laws

Reichesdorf had a courthouse, but no jail. Romanian officials some-times made arrests and took people to a jail in the nearest city. However, they could be bribed easily. For the most part, Saxons governed themselves with the guidance of the minister. Punishments involved publicly shaming the lawbreaker. For example, a man who had stolen his neighbor's wheel discs [farm implements for tilling soil] was made to carry them on his shoulders, march through the village with a drummer behind him, and shout "Do not steal! This is the punishment you will have to do for stealing!"

Burghüter – the Village Caretaker

Misch Alzner worked as the *Burghüter* during my growing up years. His three daughters were about the same age as my sisters and me. He lived with his family at the end of the community hall, and took care of all the village buildings and properties: church, school, kinder-garten, community hall, and cemetery. He cleaned the church so we wouldn't dirty our good Sunday clothes; trimmed the hedges, trees, and grass around the cemetery; swept and cleaned the school; filled inkbottles; and performed many other duties. He never got a day off. All the farmers gave him produce as part of his compensation.

The *Burghüter* kept the tower clock going and rang the bells. There were different bells for different purposes, such as school, worship, weddings, funerals, and fires. I remember the school bell being fast and high pitched. When Herr Alzner rang the funeral bell, everyone would come out of their house to see who had died. People donated money for bells in honor of loved ones who had passed away, or for other special memorials.

Four times a day, Herr Alzner rang certain bells to tell us the time: the morning bell at 6:00, the school bell at 7:30, the midday bell at 12:00, and the evening bell at 7:00. All the younger children had to be home by the evening bell. The kids 13 years and older could stay out until 10:00. Father was so strict I thought for a long time that that curfew bell was his doing. I was so surprised when I found out that it was one of the community laws!

Once, one of the Alzner girls took me up inside the bell tower. It was quite a scary hike up and up and up to the top. But it was worth it because I got to see all the bells!

It was quite something how Herr Alzner kept everything so nice and was always so punctual. Kids wished that *just once* he would ring the curfew bell late!

Market

Twice a year, in March and November, Reichesdorf held a big, open-air market. We had very few stores in the area and this big event gave villagers an opportunity to purchase necessities and new merchandise. Vendors poured into the market place by horse and wagon the day before, and pitched tents in case it rained. Eager children watched them set up.

The next morning, the vendors donned their nice clothes and waited for everyone to come, including people from neighboring villages. My sisters and brother and I had a lot of fun looking at all the different things for sale. People could buy hats, fabric, yarn, buttons, shoes, knives, dishes, utensils, pots, pans, noodle machines, toys, candy, and all kinds of other things. The adults would try to bargain. Mother and Father gave each of us kids a little money and we had to check everything out carefully to make sure we bought the very best. I really liked the candy whistles. A couple of days later, farmers filled up the market place with animals for a livestock sale.

Raising Children

Births

Our parents told us kids that a stork brought the babies. We believed this because Romania had a lot of storks, and a stork stands prominently in the Reichesdorf coat of arms. For a few years, some storks even had their nest on the community center roof! But, eventually, I started figuring things out. When Mother's maid, who was married to the year-round hired hand, got pregnant, I asked Mother, "Where will that baby come out? Through the navel? If it comes out the other place, down below, it will get all stinky and dirty." (Only animals were born that way.) Mother's whole face turned very red! I don't think she ever answered my question.

There were two midwives in the village of Reichesdorf. Since the nearest doctor was six kilometers (almost four miles) away in Birthalm, and the hospital 16 kilometers (ten miles) away in Mediasch, women gave birth at home. A short time before a baby's due date, a midwife checked on the mother daily. She would also check on the mother and baby for a few days after the birth. Mother stayed in bed for a couple of weeks after each baby was born, and Grandmother came to help look after the younger children. Relatives and neighbors brought us their best food. Each of them tried to out-do the others, so it was a good time for the older children.

Kindergarten

Children started going to Kindergarten at three years old and continued until seven years old. It began as soon as work started outside in the fields, in March or April, and would go through the harvest in October. Classes lasted all day, Monday through Saturday. The women's club hired the teacher and two assistants, and also purchased craft supplies and toys. For a while, the mothers took turns cooking the noon meal at the school for the children. But, because of farming demands, they were not able to continue. That's when they started sending sack lunches to school with each child.

There were huge sand piles in the Kindergarten yard. In good weather, the children used wheelbarrows and wooden shovels to make sand castles and bake sand cakes. They also played a lot of circle games in the yard, sometimes with a ball. When the weather turned bad, they stayed inside, creating works of art with glue, paper, and scissors. The teacher taught songs and read stories. She led prayers before and after eating. Naptime followed lunch. The children were well cared for while the mothers were out working. They had a wonderful time in Kindergarten.

While my sister Sinni went to Kindergarten, I watched the cows out in the fields. When my chores were done, I'd run as fast as I could to be home before Sinni arrived. As soon as she saw me, she burst out in a smile. If she got home and no one was there, she would cry and I would feel so bad. I didn't want her to be afraid.

Elementary School

The Saxon schools went up to eighth grade. (My brother Hans, however, went on to study at the School of Agriculture in Mediasch.)

In Reichesdorf, a new school class started every other year. Because my birthday was September 13th, I turned six after the cut-off date and had to wait two more years to start first grade. I was impatient to carry my blackboard down the street to school like the big kids! When I finally started first grade, I was eight and one of the oldest in my grade, bigger than most and one of the fastest runners.

We bought our own books for school and handed them down from one sibling to the next. At first, we wrote with chalk on our little blackboards. Each blackboard was about 10" x 12", had a wooden frame with a hole in it, and a string tied through the hole. The string also held a rag and a sponge. We would erase with the sponge and dry with the rag. Then, we graduated to pencils and paper, and even ink. We always used both sides of the paper, so as not to waste it.

A lady teacher taught the first and second grades. She sat up front and showed us how to write each letter on the classroom black-board. The blackboard had lines on it, for practicing how to write. I had already practiced at home with my sisters, but some kids had trouble staying between the lines. I liked writing and singing and playing best. They also taught us arithmetic and German. Although we spoke, read, and wrote German in school, we still spoke Såksesch at home.

For some activities the boys and girls were separated. The girls learned how to patch and sew, and later to crochet, knit, and embroider. The boys learned things like how to weave baskets and make brushes. They also got physical education. After the first trimester, we received report cards. "10" was the best score. I got 8s, 9s, and 10s.

Our third grade teacher was a man. He taught us reading, writing, arithmetic, history, speaking, singing, and Romanian. I didn't like Romanian very much. On Mondays, Rev. Herberth taught a religion class. Later on, throughout our seventh and eighth grades, we had him a lot for confirmation classes.

Students went home at noon for lunch Monday through Friday. Saturday, teachers only held school half the day.

Sometimes the school would have a program where we sang songs and recited poems from memory. The older classes put on plays for the community during the winter.

Special Memories

Christmas

The four Sunday evenings before Christmas, we got to go to school in the dark. I thought this was very special! We sang songs and lit Advent candles in wreaths we'd made in class – one for each grade.

We set up our Christmas tree in the cold room, decorated it with candies and nuts in fancy cutout paper holders, and clipped real candles onto the branches with clothespins.

On Christmas Eve, everyone fed their animals early and headed for church. The hired help had gone home for the holiday and my father had to feed the animals. All the school kids went to the school in the evening again, but then marched class-by-class to the church and sat near the sanctuary's large Christmas tree. It shined prettily with real candles on its branches. Mother, Father, and Sinni sat with all the other families. During the worship service, some of us recited poems and each class sang a song. At the end, the teachers gave every school child a basket full of gifts: pencils, erasers, and *Lebkuchen* (a holiday cake.)

Afterward, my family and I gathered at home with our relatives. We all got to eat the many cookies Mother had made. Father burned sugar and made rum for tea. All the children lined up and each recited a prayer. Then, the adults took the candy and nuts off the Christmas tree and passed them around. They'd put presents under the tree, mostly unwrapped, and Father handed them out to us kids. We usually got socks and handkerchiefs.

One year, I wanted ice skates for Christmas, but was too afraid to ask Father for them. Mother wouldn't say if there was any chance I'd get them. So, I sat down and wrote a letter to Santa Claus: "Dear Christmas Man, please bring me ice skates." I left this conspicuously in the loom and waited. Of course, I was really hoping I'd get the skates, but tried to be prepared in case I didn't. To my great surprise, on Christmas, there they were! They weren't brand new, but nice, with two width adjustments. I screwed the clamps onto my shoes and headed out for the snow and ice-covered yard. Over and over again I slipped and fell. My cousins came out from time to time to check on my progress. They'd watch me "plant potatoes" for a while and then go back in. Later, I realized I should have stayed in the house; I could never have conquered ice skating in one night, and I missed out on playing with my cousins.

Between 8:00 and 9:00 on Christmas night, we'd hear cowbells outside the house and get very excited and nervous. The Christmas Men were coming! (They were really confirmed young men walking to each house, dressed in white, wearing masks, and carrying cowbells.) If we kids could recite our prayers for them, they would give us candy. If we didn't know our prayers, they would spank us. One Christmas, my Aunt Anna Untch from America was visiting. When she heard the cowbells, she screamed and ran under the table. All the other adults laughed. *Anna Tant* was always doing crazy things like that: laughing loudly and squealing with fear or delight just for fun.

At midnight, the music teacher and some musicians climbed up into the bell tower, while all the Reichesdorfers gathered in the market place below. One musician blew a horn out through one of the tower windows. Then they all sang *A Child was Born in Bethlehem*. They repeated this in all four windows, pointing a different direction each time. It sounded so lovely in the cold night air.

Easter

Easter was as exciting as Christmas, with lots of colors and good smells. A week before, on Palm Sunday, we girls would stay inside our houses and pretend not to see the boys outside hanging evergreen branches on our house gables. We'd peek out and watch, however!

Sometimes, Father would help the boy dragging his branches up a high ladder to our gable. Later, my sisters and cousins and I would walk through the village and admire all the evergreen decorations. It was important to have very nice branches on your house! The largest and most special branches likely had been hung by a boyfriend or special admirer to the girl living there.

We colored our eggs on Good Friday by bundling them in material stuffed with flowers, onion peels, leaves, and grass and then boiling them.

Early Easter morning, before church, we visited our aunts, uncles, cousins, and grandparents to wish them a Happy Easter. Mother, as did all the other women in the village, carried a bouquet of violets or narcissus to church to hold during worship.

Easter Monday, also called "Second Easter Day," we got up early like all the other households with girls, and waited in great anticipation for a knock on our door. The boys in our classes came with perfume, either bought or homemade out of orange peels and violets. They sprinkled each of us girls on the head. Sometimes, the younger boys got carried away and our heads got soaked! We gave each of them a colored egg and a baked treat.

The fun continued on into the afternoon when all the kids gathered in circles and took turns being blindfolded, spinning around, and trying to hit an egg on the ground with a stick. Later, the confirmed youth got to go to the community hall for a dance that lasted until dawn. A Gypsy band played, teachers chaperoned, and families came to watch. The more the Gypsies drank, the better they played. Oh, how I wanted to go! Mother told me that my time would come. She had no way of knowing then that "my time" would be ripped away from me.

CHAPTER 5

War

Hitler Jugend – Hitler Youth

Hitler came into full power when I was six years old. I remember seeing posters about him and hearing about political meetings Father organized. When I was about twelve, my teacher appointed me the *Fuhrerin* (Girl Guide) for the *Hitler Jugend* (Hitler Youth.) I was to learn the lessons and songs and return home to teach my classmates. The *Jugend* camps met ten miles away in Mediasch, the nearest city. Youth gathered there for a couple of days at a time and stayed overnight in a building with bunk beds. The camp was all girls; I'm not sure where the boys' camp was, or if any boys from Reichesdorf went. The *Jugend* counselors came from around the region.

I was very scared about my first night away from home and didn't want to go *at all*. But, because my teacher had told me to go, I had to go, and often. Mother worried about me.

We wore uniforms: white blouses and blue skirts. There were probably many activities, mostly to teach us to be leaders, but I only remember learning songs and playing games. I enjoyed these, but today I'm ashamed of the ridiculous things we sang. One song had some words about shaving a grandmother. Such silly songs!

One time, the counselors dismissed us in the afternoon. Most people stayed at the camp and left in the morning. However, the sun was shining and I had my bike. So, I followed a wagon with horses out of the city. After a while I passed the wagon because I was in a hurry. It got darker and darker. There was no moon and it became extremely hard to see the road. I ran into the ditch more than once. But I didn't give up; I wanted to get home! Mother was *very* surprised to see me. Just imagine: her precious little girl alone on the road in the dark!

Back at school, our *Jung Madl* (Young Girl) group met on Saturdays after school. I led them in the songs and games I'd learned in Mediasch.

War

War came on gradually. First we heard whispers and rumors of things stirring in Germany. Then, we heard reports and speeches by Hitler on our radio. Not many people had radios in the village, so a lot of neighbors would join us to listen. Oh how Hitler's voice used to bellow! People had mixed feelings about him, just like they would of any other political leader. We didn't know about the atrocities of his reign until long after.

Germany invaded Poland September 1, 1939, instigating WWII in Europe. I was almost thirteen. Romania didn't get involved right away. When rumors and radio news reported people being burned alive, no one could believe it. The accounts were just too terrible to be real.

A year and a half later, in June 1941, when I was fourteen, Romania joined Germany in an attack against the Soviet Union, marching directly into the war effort. Soon after, we were required to take our radios to the courthouse. One day I was gathering wood from the woodshed, singing as usual, and my Aunt Anna (Greger) Gross came into the yard and said, "How can you *sing* at a time like this?" That's how I learned that Reichesdorf's men were being called to serve. Two of my cousins, Adolf Jr. Untch and Samuel Jr. Untch had to go. So did Father's cousin Sara's son, Johann Waffenschmidt.

A Funeral

July 1, 1941, one week after Romania had joined the war, the funeral bell rang for my grandfather, Andreas Greger. The Neighborhood Father and other men from his neighborhood went to the church to get a big bench to lay his body on. They put him in the middle of his cold room and we all came around to visit. I was afraid of dead people. I told Mother I'd go, but I was *not* going to look! The next day, people brought a casket for him from Mediasch. Members of his neighborhood group dug the grave.

The dead were not embalmed in those days. People wrapped their deceased in bedding and placed the body in a casket. They placed Grandfather's casket in his courtyard for the funeral ceremony. Friends and family came to pay their last respects and Rev. Herberth conducted the service. The church band played a sad song, then led all of us to the cemetery, playing horns most of the way. There, Rev. Herberth said a prayer. Everyone watched as the neighborhood men lowered the casket and filled the grave with dirt. Over the next few days, we planted flowers in the fresh dirt and placed a stone marker at the head. The graves usually had a cement border put around them, raising the level of the flowers from the path. Later, when many families were moving to Germany, they put cement slabs over the graves because no one would be left to care for them.

Changes

Our lives changed very much in those days. Prices went up and things were rationed, like coffee and sugar. We didn't get a lot of sweets. At one point, German tanks drove right into the middle of the village. So many tanks! They filled up the street! Soldiers poured into Reichesdorf and surrounding villages in preparation to fight off the Russians. They stayed in people's homes. Our family took in several, freeing up one of the bedrooms for them.

The German soldiers got a real kick out of how we washed clothes. They even made fun of the women as they worked. In Germany, the women were more advanced: they had scrubbing boards.

Me, about 16 years old
The picture on the left had been buried with other treasured possessions during the war. The spots are from moisture & mold.

A School Graduate

I finished eighth grade, the last year of school in Reichesdorf, during the war when I was sixteen. Others in my class were younger, depending on when they had started first grade. Our graduation ceremony included a celebration of our church confirmation. The regalia were very strange: full, gathered skirts; lots of ornate embroidery; and funny hats. The teachers gave each of us a certificate. Afterward, we felt grown up, since we were then allowed to do privileged things, like sit in the adult areas at church and go to the youth dances.

This step into adulthood, however, was a bittersweet affair: all the fun things we'd been looking forward to doing were abandoned because of the war. There were no more youth dances I'd dreamed of going to. All the older boys were off to the war and we didn't want to take the time to teach the boys our age how to dance; boys were slower to learn than girls.

My cousin Johanna Untch's wedding to Dolf Nemenz was consequently a small, uneventful celebration. She didn't have the traditional engagement activities with her fiancé and bridesmaids; the contributions of food by the whole community; or the hours of feasting and dancing afterward.

At Christmas, because there weren't enough young men left in Reichesdorf, my girlfriends and I dressed up as Christmas Men so the little children wouldn't be disappointed.

Post Graduate

Once I'd graduated, Father thought it would be good for me to have different experiences. He had a friend in Krohnstadt, (now *Broşov*) over 100 miles southeast from Reichesdorf. The friend was an officer in the Army and I went to work for his family while he was away on duty. He came home a couple of times, so I met him, but I was mostly with his wife and three cute children. A fourth was born while I was there. People joked that every time he came home, he and his wife had another baby nine months later.

The wife was from Germany and the family was pretty well off. They had a phone in their house and all of them wore nice clothes. They even had a flush toilet! It was my job to clean and to watch the children, who were all under five years old. They paid me in room and board and gave me Sunday afternoons off. The work was okay; I didn't mind it. But I liked farming better.

The woman would send me out after dark for groceries. I was *terrified*. I'd walk cautiously around the corner, and then take off like a blitz. Once, I thought someone was following me. It's a good thing my employer didn't have a long grocery list!

One of my friends, Regina Wachsmann, worked for a neighbor in Krohnstadt, across the street and a couple of houses up from me. We got together once in a while on the weekends. I washed dishes so slowly that she would take over washing dishes so we could go have fun.

When my employer was pregnant and preparing for labor, she prearranged for Regina to come with me to get the midwife for the birth. When that time came, we ran as fast as we could go. The Romanian police thought we were criminals or illegal immigrants or something, and they apprehended us outside the midwife's house. We called to the midwife from the street so she would know it was time for the baby. She called Regina's employer and he came to the courthouse to untangle the mess we were in. Romanian police were so foolish!

Father called to tell me he was being sent away to train Romanian soldiers. (He was 52 and had *not* expected to have to serve again.) The Romanian Navy sent him south to train young seaman near the Black Sea. Under his command, the men practiced marching, but they had to use sticks as there were no extra guns.

Krohnstadt was an important city: the county capital and a major center for transportation. On Easter Sunday, the Romanian army was celebrating the holiday instead of keeping watch. I was in my employer's garden and heard planes coming. I had no idea what was going on. Then bombs dropped on the railroad depot right there in Krohnstadt.

From then on, whenever bombers were approaching, the city's warning sirens went off and we would run to a neighbor's underground bunker. There were many false alarms, which became unnerving. Some of them sounded too late for us to even take cover! Finally, we left the city with a group of the family's friends and traveled to a camp in the woods, far from the enemy's targets in Krohnstadt.

While at the camp, I got a letter from my Grandmother. She said that with Father gone and the hired help also drafted into the war, Mother was having a hard time keeping up with the farm. The people I worked for understood the problem and let me go.

I rode the train as far as Mediasch, almost 100 miles, and then walked the final ten miles. Close to Reichesdorf, I saw people pulling thistles out of the grain near the road. It was Mother and Uncle Fritz! There was also a Russian POW with them who'd been assigned to work for our family. There were no emotional greetings or hugs; those years of war were somber ones. We weren't an affectionate people, either. Our family expressed love by working hard and helping each other. So, I just got right to work, pulling thistles alongside them until we finished the weeding and went home. Today, I regret not hugging my mother more.

Day after day, without Father and the hired hands, we worked long, long hours to keep the farm running.

Prisoner Of War

Only the larger farms had POW hands because the farmers had to pay them room and board and a little extra. Our Russian POW didn't speak German or Såksesch, so it was difficult to communicate with him. He did speak a little Romanian, however, and the Romanians knew a little Russian. We learned that he had a wife and children back in Russia. I didn't feel uncomfortable with him around.

Mother treated everyone on our farm the same: POW, hired hands, and family members. She fed the Russian along with everyone else and didn't worry about him running away. Where was he to go? On Sundays, she gave him a bottle of wine to keep him entertained while we were at church. "When hands are happy, they work harder," she said.

Almost a year after Father had been sent to train seamen, some good Riesling and distilled liquor got him an early release and he came home to us. Romanians were so easy to bribe! Father hoped that Germany would win and annex Romania, because he was so disillusioned with the Romanian government.

I was more relieved than happy to see him. Again, it was war; we didn't know how to be happy. We didn't know if or when he would be taken away from us again.

Too Close

In 1943, when I was seventeen, the Russians and their allies started attacking cities near Reichesdorf. We could hear their guns and bombs from home. The front was very close and I was very scared!

Some of the Russian soldiers would steal Romanians' horses and ride all over the country scaring people. We slept in our barns or far from our houses to hide from them. One woman gave birth while hiding out in a field.

People did some weird things during those times. They weren't allowed guns so they felt powerless. The older generations, like my parents, had already lived through a major war; they knew what to fear. Some people committed suicide. An old couple in the village hung themselves. Everyone started burying possessions that could be dug back up when the fighting was over. We buried a barrel of beans, canned pork, linens and towels, valuables, documents, and photographs. Some things were ruined by mold.

On August 23, 1944, a governmental coup resulted in an overthrow of the Romanian regime. The new regime signed a peace treaty with the Soviets. Then they aligned themselves with the Allies and turned to fight against the Germans. In that move, we Saxons lost all our rights. After eight hundred years of governing ourselves, our special privileges were ripped away from us.

World War II brought devastation and disappointment to our beautiful Transylvanian Siebenburgen. Romania broke its long-standing promises to the Saxons and we would never live peaceably or profitably in our own country again.

Personal Consequences

Up until this point, my life had been wonderful. If the war hadn't come, I would have been a normal teenager, going wild like any other young person. I would have gone to dances, told stories, and played jokes on my friends.

Perhaps I might have stayed in Krohnstadt, or gone away to school and become a teacher. Or, I might have stayed on the farm. I loved the farm and working in the garden. I was good with green houses. Most likely, I would have eventually done as my mother did: keep house, raise children, and farm in Romania. Instead, when I turned sixteen, my world crumbled; any dreams I might have had for myself in Romania ended.

Two of my boy cousins lost their chances for *any* future; the war claimed both their lives. Adolf Untch left behind his wife, Anna, and their two little girls. Samuel Untch was only 17. Their bodies were never brought home.

Samuel Untch Jr.

Adolf Untch Jr.

CHAPTER 6

Soviet Labor Camp

War Criminals

In January 1944, I was eighteen years old. Kathi was almost 25, Yinni 21, Hans 14, and Sinni 7. There were rumors of an impending deportation, but we didn't know what to think about it because no one had ever heard of such a thing before. Supposedly, the Soviets were going to take the younger adult Saxons off to work in the USSR. It was hard to believe anyone would allow this to happen. Nevertheless, the younger people hid in dugouts in the forest and moved frequently to elude any searchers. My parents butchered a pig, canned it, and buried it in the woods. Then, they sent me and my two older sisters, loaded with provisions, into the woods to hide. We started to dig a bunker into the hillside.

About this time, the Romanian authorities called a meeting at the community hall. Father went and learned that all able-bodied German men ages 17 to 45, who had not already been taken into the army, and able-bodied German women ages 18 to 30, were to be taken to the USSR to make war reparations. The idea was that, since

Germans had caused the war, Germans were going to rebuild what had been destroyed. They were to serve for five years. However, if the Saxons tried to evade the deportation, soldiers would take the older adults and younger children instead. My sisters and I were only beginning to dig our bunker when Father came to tell us it was no use, we had to go.

Meanwhile, Mother had prepared two homemade backpacks filled with blankets, flannel clothing, food, and whatever else we could carry. She was waiting in the yard for us, holding the backpacks. Little Sinni stood by her side, eyes wide open in disbelief. Mother handed the backpacks to Kathi and me and told us to hurry and catch up with the others already leaving.

Yinni didn't go with us; Father figured she wouldn't be sent to the camps because of her bad feet. We loaded our backpacks onto wagons and walked behind the other "able-bodied" Reichesdorfers, all numb in a state of shock. This couldn't possibly be happening!

My cousin Johanna (Untch) Nemenz, now a wife and mother, walked with us as well. Her husband, Dolf, had stayed in the Romanian army, so she had to leave their one-year-old daughter, Susi, with her mother. All mothers with children over a year old had to go. Johanna was lucky in a way; there was a woman from Birthalm who had seven children and no relatives to leave her children with. They ended up with one of her neighbors.

My Uncle Fritz Greger (Mother's brother) was also taken, but with a group rounded up a few days later. This was the Uncle Fritz who used to take us to the dentist with his horses Otto and Batar. His oldest, Gretel, was my age and in school with me, but a little too young in 1945 to be deported.

That winter, some 30,000 Transylvanian Saxons were deported to the USSR to work in forced labor camps. January 14, 1945, as Kathi, our cousins, neighbors, and I walked out of the village, the church funeral bells rang out. I was afraid I wouldn't see Mother and

Father again for five years. It was a good thing I couldn't see what my future would really entail.

A Long Way to Ukraine

We walked ten miles to the school in Mediasch, and slept on the floor for two nights. The officers had a terrible time deciding how to divide us into groups before loading us into railroad box cars. Our parents came to see us, but weren't allowed in; we were already imprisoned.

Father brought us more clothing and coats for the cold and had to pass them through a window. We could talk to him, but not hug him. He couldn't comfort us. It was heartbreaking.

Finally, they loaded us into the box cars, each group headed for a different destination. We were lucky to have so many of us related. They let Kathi and me stay together, along with some of our cousins: Johanna (Untch) Nemenz, Katharina (Untch) Kloos, Johanna (Hanni) Untch, Regina Waffenschmidt, and Regina Jr. Greger.

The box cars had benches for us to sit on, but no other luxuries. By the time we got to the Ukraine border, (maybe a week later) our packed foods were gone. They brought us soup when we transferred to a Soviet train. It was not tasty. But later, as we grew hungrier, we were very sorry we didn't eat it.

At least the Soviet trains were bigger and nicer: double decker with bunk beds. The toilet, however, was merely a hole in the middle of the floor. A group of people would hold up blankets for privacy when someone had to go to the bathroom.

Farther into the USSR, the train *finally* made its first stop and the soldiers opened the doors. Everyone rushed out to relieve themselves away from the little hole. But, there were no bushes to hide behind! We kept running and running, looking for cover, with the soldiers yelling at us and chasing us. Finally, we just squatted in front of each other and the soldiers. But, we were *not* happy about it;

it was humiliating. We grabbed snow to wash ourselves, not having bathed since before we'd left home.

We spent a total of two weeks on these trains, talking to each other, worrying, and occasionally singing. *Surely*, we thought, someone would rescue us. Surely, this horrible fate could not be allowed to happen!

The train's final destination was Konstantinovka, in Ukraine. We arrived there on February 2, 1945. From the hill above Konstantinovka, you could see the smokestacks of Kiev. We didn't know we were in Ukraine. The whole time we spent in the labor camps, we thought we were in Russia. Our train ride had seemed long enough to have taken us that far. The Ukrainian language sounded like Russian. I suppose there were Russian soldiers mixed in with Ukrainian soldiers.

The Russians had an oppressive control over Ukraine and the other Soviet countries. Later, when I had access to a map, I figured out that we had been in Ukraine, instead.

Ukraine

Welcome to the Labor Camp

We had to walk five kilometers (three miles) carrying our belongings from the depot to Camp Number 1048. Some had suitcases, which they dragged behind them in the snow. The soldiers led us to an old, bombed-out building that had been converted into barracks. It had no heat, just bunk beds made of boards nailed together. There wasn't even any straw for us to put on the boards for mattresses. *Surely, this must be temporary housing*, we thought.

The first thing they did was to divide us into groups, some to take to the showers, and others to the river to break ice with crowbars. The river crew had to pull the broken ice up with hooks and load it into trucks. The soldiers and our people hauled the ice into an insulated cellar. We didn't know what it was to be used for.

During these first weeks, the Ukrainians took us to see a couple of their dance performances. They wanted us to experience some of their culture, I guess. Later, we would be too dirty and too tired to take anywhere.

After two weeks, they sent 180 of us from Camp Number 1048 to the Sofos, a state farm. They divided us into brigades of 12 to 15 people, each supervised by a brigadier. Some brigades were assigned to rebuild homes in town. Others were chosen for factories or wherever else they were needed. Kathi, our cousins, (Johanna, Katharina, and Hanni) and I were in a brigade selected to work acres and acres of vegetable crops.

Life in Camp

All 180 of us stayed in a barn with a cement floor and two rows of bunk beds. The eight men in the group slept in one corner. There was a stove in the middle, but no fuel to burn in it. Katharina and I huddled together at night with our two blankets: Kathi's blanket we folded over to soften the bed, and my blanket we used for cover.

Our bathroom facilities consisted of a large ditch with two boards across and a fence around for "privacy." We had to squat. There was no running water either, to drink or wash with.

The kitchen was in the same building as the barracks, but a completely separate room. Only Ukrainians worked in the kitchen. Our meals – two a day – included cabbage soup, a piece of bread, and a spoonful of wheat mush (hot cereal.) I guess the mush was our dessert. If we were lucky, they put a little sunflower oil on top of it. Oh, how tasty that was! The cooks however, often took the oil home with them instead of giving it to us. They were starving, too.

We always had a brigadier, a Soviet man (or sometimes a woman) with a gun over his shoulder, watching us and telling us where to go and what to do. He would yell at us to work faster or hurry up. Now and then, a higher officer came to tell him where we were needed. The women brigadiers were easier on us than the men. They would touch our clothing and say, "Berlin!

Berlin!" They thought we were from the big city in Germany and were admiring the material of our skirts and coats.

At first, we had a translator, whom we called "*Zoder*," which means "rag," because her clothes were ragged. It didn't take long to catch on to the daily language and the more Ukrainian we learned, the less we believed what she said. Zoder didn't always tell us the truth. She was, however, just another Soviet, trying to make things better for herself.

Hunger got to be a normal feeling for us. We grew very skinny, and made up funny songs about ourselves, such as one about our pants barely hanging on. In the fall, when we were harvesting tomatoes, we ate as many tomatoes as we could in the field. This filled our bellies but cut down on the amount of sleep we got; we had to run to the "facilities" up to ten times a night. Because of the stress and lack of nourishment, our periods stopped shortly after we arrived. This was fortunate, since we had no way to wash.

Also, it was so cold we didn't undress all winter. Every day we walked about two miles to the fields, wrapped in our blankets to keep from freezing. Kathi and I had each brought a pair of long pants to wear under our skirts in the cold, and one change of clothing. The change of clothing, however, served as a second layer for warmth, and we didn't take it off until spring.

In the fields, we huddled behind things, like irrigation pipes, to get out of the biting cold wind. I remember thinking about Jesus' suffering and comparing it to mine. At least I wasn't bleeding.

Hunger and cold weren't our only troubles, though. One time I saw a woman picking through another woman's hair. I asked someone what they were doing. "Picking out the lice," she said. After that, all of us lined up, one behind another, picking through each other's hair for lice.

From time to time, an army officer conducted an inspection. He would go through all our belongings, usually when we were out in the fields. After one inspection, I noticed that my good comb was missing, one with teeth close enough to comb out lice. I had to use Kathi's after that. Later, she contacted a factory worker who made combs on the side. He made me one that had "Konstantinovka" printed on it, along with my name and the date.

Our guards weren't abusive, only mean and loud when telling us to finish a job. Sometimes it felt like they saw us as animals, not as human beings. Workers did try to escape, but they were just caught and put back to work. There really wasn't any place for us to run, anyway. The soldiers got more and more lax as time went on. They were suffering too: hungry and cold just like us.

We got pretty lonesome for our families. But, fortunately, there were so many of us relatives and friends together: sisters, cousins, and others from our village. We felt sorry for the Ukrainians who worked alongside us in the fields. They didn't own anything, not even the land they had to work; everything belonged to the government. They were starving, too. In war, it's always the poorest who suffer the most. Some were compassionate and felt sorry for us. They taught us to steal: how to stuff food in our shirts and pants so it wouldn't be noticed, and how to slip flat, misshapen potatoes inside our shoes, under our heels.

The First Winter

That first winter in the fields, the supervisors gave us crowbars to break the frozen dirt loose. There were piles of it, which turned out to be frozen cabbage heads. The Ukrainians had not finished their harvesting before the winter freeze. With so many people off to war, they had been short of workers. After we pried the cabbage heads out of the ground, the Ukrainians hauled them to a storage facility.

On our next assignment, we prepared garden hotbeds. First, we shoveled and carted dried manure on wooden stretchers and dumped it into wooden frames on the ground. On top of the manure, we layered dirt. Next, the Ukrainian women planted seeds. We then enclosed the wooden box with glass windows and placed straw mats on top of those. They had straw for the plants, but not for our beds!

The Ukrainian women tended the prepared hotbeds. They opened and closed the windows and moved the straw mats as needed to regulate the temperature. The field officer found other work for us.

I wore out my only pair of shoes walking around in the slush all winter. Our brigadier, a little man, gave me a pair of galoshes – low rubber boots with no insulation. They were too big, so I wrapped rags around my feet to keep them warm and to make the galoshes fit better.

Saving Kathi

After a few months at the Sofos, Kathi got sick. I came back from work one day, and she was gone; they had taken her to the hospital. An officer gave me a permit to miss work and visit her. The nurses made me put on a white coat before entering her room. She was so swollen I hardly recognized her. Part of her hospital stay, she was in a coma, and was not expected to live.

The doctor gave her an experimental shot to rid her body of the excess water. It worked, but she became very thin and weak. Her mind was okay, but her legs, arms, and hands couldn't function. She had to learn to walk, talk, and write all over again. I sold my watch to our woman brigadier (who'd had her eye on it ever since I arrived) for a good price. With the money, I bought bread for Kathi. It's funny how much that watch had meant to me. But, since we had arrived in Ukraine, there was always someone to tell us when to get up, where to go, what to do, and when to go back. It didn't matter what time it was anymore. And, the watch meant nothing compared to getting food for Kathi. I don't even remember when I got another watch. It just wasn't important any more. Family is the most important thing!

Kathi stayed in the hospital for several months. After about three weeks, the officers refused to give me a permit to miss work. However, I was determined to see my sister. Family is the most important thing in the world; I had to find a way to get to Kathi! When my brigade walked to work in the morning, followed by one of the soldiers, I would get near the front of the group and disappear into a cornfield. Once everyone had passed, I'd sneak off to the hospital. In this way, I managed to visit Kathi at least once a month.

My cousin Regina Nemenz (Aunt Regina Greger-Nemenz' daughter) worked in the Zink Factory about four miles from where I was staying. She was also able to visit Kathi in the hospital.

Lice and Typhus

We soon learned that head lice weren't the only kind of lice; some lived in clothing or beds and some lived on other parts of the body. In late spring, when the weather got warm, we found lice on our heads and in our clothes. It was as if they were coming out of the ground. Consequently, typhus broke out. Anyone that got typhus was taken to the hospital, where their heads were shaved and they were treated. Many died from the fever. My cousin, Regina Waffenschmidt, (our Untch grandmothers were sisters) was one who had lice and got sick. She was Kathi's age and had lived in a village near Reichesdorf. I saw her in the hospital once when I visited my sister. They had shaved her head. We talked for a little while.

The Ukrainians started bringing barrels of water by the barracks, so we had some to drink and to wash our faces with. But, we didn't have any way to wash our clothes. In the summer, someone found a stream where we could do laundry, if we weren't too tired.

Trips to Town

Because of the lice and the diseases they carried, the soldiers started giving us Sundays off to take showers and have our clothes cleaned. We had to walk five miles into town to do this. The washing place was a building with a long line of showers and an oven for the clothes, which got hot enough to kill lice and their eggs. A man tended the oven while we showered. Sometimes, the oven fire wasn't hot enough and we had to wait naked a long time for the clothes to get done. We didn't have extra changes of clothes. I had two skirts, but although it was warmer, I had to wear both of them at the same time to cover all the holes. As we sat naked, the man didn't look at us any differently than he would a stick of wood.

After washing, we would sell bread at a bazaar in town. Although we needed the bread too, it was all we had to sell. We always got something for it, mushy and under-baked as it was; everyone was hungry there. Often, we traded for yogurt or eggs. We longed for milk and eggs because they never gave us any at the camp. Once, when we'd earned a little money, we used it to buy another comb to get the lice out of our hair.

News of Family and Friends

Sometimes, Saxons would be taken to work somewhere else, temporarily. They would come back with news of friends and relatives that they'd seen. My cousin, Johanna, worked with trucks that transported grain for cattle. They would haul the grain to different places. Six months after our arrival in Ukraine, she came upon some of our people. She learned that my sister Yinni, whom we had last seen in Mediasch, had been taken after all. Soldiers had picked her up just a couple of days after us and shipped her off to a Soviet coal mine. There was no getting out of the labor camps, for flat feet or anything else.

The first time we got a letter from Father, it was a big event in the barracks. I have no idea how he got our address. Everyone wanted to hear the letter and begged us to read it out loud. The letters were censored, but we were able to read that Grandmother, Rosina Greger, had died (July 3, 1945) at the age of 67. How frustrating and sad that we couldn't have been there for the funeral!

Father said they had enough to eat, that they wondered how we were, and he asked us to write. Sometimes, the brigadier would tell us that if we got a certain amount of work done, he would give us cards to write home. We worked very hard, finished all the jobs, but never got any cards. They often lied to us like that. Consequently, I was not able to write Father back while I was in Ukraine.

Kathi is Shipped Out

In August or September, when Kathi was well enough to travel, the Soviets shipped her to Delitzsch, East Germany. She was among the first group transported out of the camp because they were too weak to work. I received a card from her with her address. Of course, without stationary, I couldn't reply. Fortunately, I kept the card; a year and a half later, it turned out to be very important to my survival.

Chicken Dinners

The second winter, the Soviets built some barracks for us with a stove in the middle. They even gave us coal to burn! And, luxuries of luxuries, we got straw mattresses. All the bunk beds were nailed together in a long row, the length of the building.

They took us to work in a brick building this time, to construct straw mats for the hotbeds. We made the mats by tying bunches of straw to strings hanging down from a frame. At the other end of the building was a chicken coop, with chicken wire separating our piles of straw from the chickens.

One day, someone noticed an egg in the straw. The fence had a hole in it and the hens were coming through to lay eggs. What a happy situation for us! We really missed eggs. One day, I saw a hen in the straw. Remembering a trick from childhood, I put her head under her wing and rocked her to sleep by swinging my arms like a pendulum. Then, I stuffed her in my flannel pants, under my skirt and tied my pant leg with a string. Friends kept close around me for cover as I walked back to the barracks with a sleeping chicken in my pants. All the workers knew about it.

I had done my part, catching and carrying the chicken. At the barracks, my cousin Johanna Untch Nemenz took over. Since we had a stove and hot water now, she butchered the chicken and added some coarsely ground cattle feed to stretch the meal. My cousins and I had a feast!

After a while, more and more chickens escaped into the straw, and ended up in the laborers' pots.

Unfortunately, this didn't last. The chickens were eventually moved to the other side of the stream and we lost our chicken dinners.

Potatoes and Sugar Beets

Toward the second spring, our supervisors took us to huge, potato-filled cellars and had us sort potatoes for seed. We always tucked away a few potatoes to bring back to the barracks. If someone got too greedy, the brigadier would notice and frisk us. Here we were, sitting amongst all these potatoes, starving to death! Some people were so desperate that they hid potatoes in the bucket we'd been given to pee in. They'd tell us not to do anything "big" in the bucket, only pee. When it was time to dump the bucket, they would grab the potatoes and take them home. I never did use the bucket to sneak food home, but it proved how bad things had gotten and how desperate people were to survive. Eventually, the guards caught on and the only potatoes we could sneak out were flat ones hidden in the heel of our shoes. We would walk all the way back to the barracks on our toes.

Some people worked with sugar beets. They would sneak some back to the barracks and bake them in the coals. I found one on the road that had fallen off a truck, and grabbed it to take back with me. It was so good! If sugar beets tasted so good, why in Reichesdorf did we only feed them to the cows? Of course, everything tastes so much better when you're starving.

Night Work

Later that second spring, we prepared the irrigation canal by shoveling out dirt and building up the sides. Then, when the hot bed plants were large enough to set out, the Ukrainians made furrows in the garden and we planted the seedlings in the furrows. As soon as we finished each row, Ukrainian women ran water from the canal into the furrows, just enough to wet the new plants. We planted acres of tomatoes and cabbage in the good, fertile soil. When it got very hot, the seedlings started to wilt before they were all in the ground. The supervisors decided that we should stay up the whole night and plant when the temperature was cooler. One of the weaker girls held a torch, and we planted tomatoes by torchlight. They made us work the whole day and night and did not give us anything to eat after lunch. Exhausted and hungry, we stumbled into the barracks the next morning, ate our ration of borscht (in this case, cabbage soup with a few beans) and kasha (buckwheat mush) and dropped into bed. We did this for about two weeks: sleeping in the day and working at night.

Harvesting

Sometimes our supervisors had us harvest other crops in addition to the ones we cared for. I remember harvesting watermelons and getting so sticky! Another time, we loaded cucumbers into a truck headed for town. We rode on top of the pile and ate them like apples.

Sick Days

I worked in the wheat harvest once, turning the wheel on a grindstone to sharpen sickles. However, I had boils on my hands and arms and the dust made them worse. The brigadiers wouldn't let me off unless I had a fever. They didn't like people lying around. Finally, after I complained hard and showed them my boils, they let me stay in the barracks for a couple of days. I spent the whole time in my bunk.

One day, a male brigadier told us that when we finished moving a large pile of grain from one storage shed to another, we could go home for the day. We worked very fast and finished much sooner than he expected. When we started to leave, he gave us another job.

By that time, we'd had enough and made a break for the barracks, running, knowing that he was too old to catch us. Instead, he sent a few Ukrainian boys after us. We kept running, up a hill, but the boys gained on us. One by one, the workers dropped off. Remembering a story my Grandmother had once told me about a girl who fainted to get out of a difficult situation, I pretend to faint. The boys were scared when they saw me lying on the ground and talked amongst themselves, trying to decide if I was sick or faking it. It had been a long, up-hill run, so I just rested and let them talk for a while. Then I came to, holding my chest. "I'm sick," I said. One of the boys knew me, from when I had worked with his mother. He said, "Let her go!" and they did. All the others had to go back to work.

Another time, a lump formed on my wrist. I showed it to the guard and told him I was sick; I couldn't shovel the dirt or manure for the hot beds. So, he gave me a break. My wrist didn't really hurt, but he didn't need to know that! We did what we had to.

Trouble in the Barracks

Our new bunk beds became infested with bed bugs. They got into the boards of the beds and, at night, would crawl out and suck our blood. The bites hurt and became infected. Some people dragged their straw mattresses out into the yard to get away from the bugs.

The barracks also had a lot of rats. I slept in a lower bunk. One night, a rat woke me up when it ran over my feet, up my body, over my face, and slipped on my nose, leaving a bloody scratch.

Eventually, the men got some gasoline and threw it on the rats, then set them on fire. With all the vermin and poor hygiene, it was no wonder so many people caught typhus.

One night, during the warm months, the long row of connected bunks started shifting, making a terrible noise. Everyone jumped off as fast as they could. Fortunately, the wall stopped the beds from totally collapsing. Parts of the structure covered the floor of the barn in a big mess, however, and we had to set up our blankets outside. I couldn't sleep out there in the open, though, not without a roof over my head. Thankfully, workers repaired the bunk beds the next day.

The Ukrainians finally built new, smaller barracks because it was impossible for us to stay in the large, infested ones. I only stayed in the new quarters a short time, however, as my fate soon changed.

Too Weak

Every so often, the weakest workers would be sent to town to face a commission of doctors and officials, mostly men. After two years and two months, our supervisors sent me. It was March 21, 1947, my third spring in Ukraine. The commission had us march naked around their table for an inspection, to see if we were fit enough to work or if we were too thin and run down. I was barely able to walk by this time. My mind was weak, too. Fortunately, they decided to cut short my five-year sentence. If they had sent me back to the work camp, I would have died.

Other People's Labor Camp Experiences

Cousin Katharina

My cousin, Katharina Untch, (Uncle Dolf's daughter) was in the labor camp with me. She stayed at the camp for three years until she was too weak to work and she was allowed to return home to Romania. Katharina offered to let her sister, Johanna Nemenz, go home in her place because Johanna missed her little girl so much. But, the Soviets told Katharina that if she didn't want to go home, they could both stay in the camp, so Katharina returned to Romania.

Regina Untch

My sister Yinni, despite her flat feet, was sent to Petrovka, Ukraine to work in a coal mine. There, the Soviets would blast tunnels through the mine and, after they had stabilized the walls, the Germans would go in and shovel coal into rail cars. They were told not to kill any rats in the mine; rats could sense when something was wrong and would run out before people even knew there was a problem. If the workers saw rats running out of the mine, they were to follow.

The Soviets had to feed the miners more than other workers, because the job was so strenuous. Even so, Yinni's health deteriorated. She became so skinny they nicknamed her "Bones." Her supervisors finally moved her into the kitchen to work, where she was allowed to eat more. If anyone left food on their plates, she got the leftovers. She lasted the whole five-year sentence and then returned to Reichesdorf.

Horst Rampelt of Mediasch

(Although we may have been in the same camp at the same time, I didn't know this man. There were so many of us and he came from a different town.)

From page 94 of *Reichesdorf*, edited by Andreas Nemenz. © 1999, Germany. Translated by Alice Melgaard Ard.

I was barely 17 years old when they took us to Russia [Ukraine]. We arrived at Konstantinovka Camp Number 1048, where we were some 1200 people in cramped quarters. Most of us came from the Mediasch region, and a few were Hungarians of German ancestry. Amongst us was a minister from Mediasch and a professor. We asked the minister if it was a sin to steal

– especially food. He replied that it was a bigger sin not to take care of your body and let it die. Hunger dictated our actions in those years. We set out and looked for food, wherever we worked or whenever the opportunity arose. Of course, not everyone had the opportunity, especially those who worked in the mines. The miners were given bigger portions of food.

The Russian people were not much better off. At least they had a garden, or worked in a kitchen. Our bowl and spoon were always with us and the soup kitchen followed us wherever we worked. Twice a day we got clear soup and once a day we got a piece of heavy bread. The first time they took us to delouse, my spoon fell out of my pants pocket and I lost it. I was devastated to have such a problem. An older man offered to sell me an extra spoon he had for twenty Rubels. It was a huge price, but I had no other way out.

The ability to communicate was very difficult at first. We tried German, Romanian, Hungarian, and hands, but we were not always understood. 1945 and 1946 passed in spite of hunger and cold, but the winter of 1946-47 surpassed all. Hunger, bugs and hard work had weakened our bodies and we had no strength left. We could see death at our door.

During the fall, we usually worked in pairs. It was 15-20 km (8-12 miles) to cornfields where we filled our backpacks to have something for our stomachs. But the winter was too long and we ran out of corn. Many lives were lost in early 1947. For a while, I worked digging graves. The ground was frozen to a depth of more than a meter. We worked with a pick, and it took a lot of swings to dig a grave because the frozen chunks were only the size of a nut. It took a whole day to dig a grave a meter deep. People were dying faster than we could open graves. So, often they put three bodies, wrapped in a sheet or blanket, into a one-meter deep grave.

Somehow, spring arrived, and those who were still able, wandered to the potato fields during the night. The potatoes were planted that day and we harvested or stole them that night. We wanted to live, to survive! Even the cats were caught and eaten, and what a delicacy!

We grew stronger as summer came. One day, eight men were picked to travel to the collective to help with the potato harvest some 20-km from camp. I was the youngest. When we arrived at the collective Schirokij-Schleach, the grain was already harvested. We were fed very well there for two weeks. We worked hard and pleased the president. It rained hard one morning and we thought about sleeping in, but it wasn't long until the brigadier stood in our sleeping quarters. He needed a few men to help clean the wheat. I volunteered because I thought of all the wheat that I would be able to take back with me. It really paid off. In the end, every one of us had 20-liter wheat under his pillow. It was a good feeling to have this extra food when we returned to the camp because the bad months were not over yet. However, the next day fear broke out when a truck came and wanted to take us to the Zinkkolchos, where they had work for us. That farm belonged to the Zink factory, which was a part of our camp. We were worried about what would happen to our wheat if we went.

After arriving at the Zinkkolchos, all we could do was ask "Why?" God had brought us here for a reason. They needed us to work and we were sent to load potatoes. This was the best possible outcome! It was as nice as Christmas and Easter combined. We ate and ate potatoes, as many as we could hold. I'm not exaggerating when I say that each of us could eat more than a bucket full of baked potatoes a day. We gained a lot of strength and a lot of pounds. We could hardly believe our good fortune.

In the middle of June 1947, a commission was to come to camp to separate out the weak workers and either send them home or to Germany. Since workers were so desperately needed, some of the undernourished ones were sent to the Zinkkolchos where the tomatoes were ripening and needed picking. Even weak workers could pick tomatoes. I was one of them and so was my future wife, Katharina Pinnes from Reichesdorf. We did not even look at each other, because our minds were on other things. We tried to quell our hunger with tomatoes. We ate so many, and we were so weak, that our stomach system could not digest properly. An epidemic broke out. God was with us, and He never left us during that horrible situation.

Never to Return

At the end of his service, the Soviets put my Uncle Fritz (Mother's brother) on a train for Germany. People saw him get on. But, he never got off. He had disappeared along the way somewhere, as well as his belongings. He wouldn't have run away. His only thoughts would have been to get home. That's what everyone wanted more than anything else. Many people died on those train rides out of the labor camps and their bodies were either tossed out of the train or buried at the border of East Germany. No one ever found out what happened to Uncle Fritz; not even a rag of his ever turned up. His wife Margarete and children: Gretel, Friedrich Jr., and Anna, didn't even have a grave to visit.

Reichesdorf Numbers of Forced Laborers

85 young women and 36 men from Reichesdorf had been deported to the Ukraine; three of the women and eleven of the men died there.

CHAPTER 7

Life for Those Back Home

Mother, Sinni, (about 8) Hans, (about 15) and Father

While the "able-bodied" Saxons were starving and slaving away for the Soviets, the people back in Reichesdorf were suffering, too. Until the end of 1945, Soviets, Romanians, and Gypsies carried out nightly searches for Saxons who had hidden and escaped deportation. They inflicted frequent punishments; our loved ones lived in constant fear.

Hiding Out

(Information gathered from *Reichesdorf*, edited by Andreas Nemenz. © 1999, Germany.)

My friend Regina Lang was six months pregnant in November 1944, when her father heard about the pending deportation. Once it was clear that no rescue was forthcoming, Herr Lang started making secret plans: he decided to build a bunker in the woods with his neighbor, Herr Luitz. The men slipped out at 3:00 in the morning to work on the bunker, and returned after nightfall. If they had been seen, they would have been arrested. After they'd finished the bunker, the Luitz family moved in on January 12, 1945. The Lang family left to move in the next day.

When the Langs got to the bunker, they couldn't believe their eyes; the Luitzs were not there and all the tools and dishes were gone. The Langs made a fire, which thawed the ground, causing the bunker to cave in. Regina was trapped in the cave-in. She started having labor contractions, but didn't tell anyone because they all had enough problems. The Langs decided to go look for the Luitz family in the nearby village, Schlatt, because that's where Herr Luitz's hired man, Schenker, lived.

They found the Luitzs in Schlatt and learned that someone had seen them, so they had left the bunker to avoid being found and arrested. The two families tried again, building a bigger bunker in a thickly forested area near Schlatt, which most people avoided because of the army deserters hiding there. It took them a week, constructing a roof out of wood this time so it wouldn't cave in on them.

Regina lost her baby girl three days after the cave-in. After the miscarriage, her mother stayed with her at the Schenker family's farm in Schlatt. They had to hide in the hayloft because Soviet soldiers were looking for people to deport. The soldiers looked in the barn and stuck bayonets in the hayloft, but luckily didn't climb up to look any closer. The next night, Mr. Schenker hid the women in his wagon, covered them with hay, and drove them to the bunker. The two families were all together now, twelve people in one room.

One of the few people who knew where they were, Regina's uncle, brought them pots and pans, a lamp and a stove. They used milk cans for water, which they got from a field well. During the winter, they melted snow for water. The women took turns cooking and the men gathered wood and water. Every week, the uncle brought them food and news. Friends took care of their animals at home. The Romanian notary, a compassionate man, even helped by putting a note on their door that said the house belonged to the government and no one was to use it.

After about three months, the two families thought it would be safe to return. Regina's parents left first to make sure. Back at their house, they found a lot of things missing, including bedding and dishes. They had learned, however, that a family didn't need a lot to get by on. How huge their house seemed after spending three months in a tiny bunker!

Terror and Loss

Up to this point, Saxons had been Germans but Romanian citizens. By 1945, they'd been labeled "war criminals" and had lost their Romanian citizenship. The Romanians hated our people. They saw the Saxons as Hitlerists and enemies of the State, and denied them political rights and voting privileges for many years. Saxon men in Germany, who had fought with the Germans, were not allowed to return to their families in Romania.

March 23, 1945, when Katharina and I had been away in Ukraine for almost two months, the Romanian government put into effect one of its agriculture reforms (an effort to redistribute the land wealth.) Romanian officials took land, homes, equipment, and live-stock away from all Germans living in Romania and redistributed it among the Romanians. Over time, 60,000 Saxons were forced to leave their farms. The towns lost over 50 percent of their lands and the Church 55 percent. The government placed city industries and banks under State control and "disowned" tradesmen and merchants; meaning they took business men's rights and properties, including their homes.

Romanian officials would bring a slip of paper to a house and take a cow, or a pig, wine, or equipment. Everything belonged to the State, they said. There was no democratic process and no individual rights, as is often the case in Communist governments. Father said, "We are homeless in our own homes."

The Romanians and Gypsies established town commissions. Reichesdorf had 17 men in its commission: 10 Romanians and 7 Gypsies. They ruled with force and brutality, beating and humiliating the Saxons who wouldn't give up their property.

The villagers were terrorized daily. In one case, a drunken Romanian policeman, along with a group of drunken Gypsies, ordered two Saxon neighbors to fight each other. When the neighbors didn't hit hard enough, the Romanian threatened them with his gun. When the neighbors finally beat each other bloody, the group was satisfied and left.

In another instance, a bunch of Gypsies showed up to a school dance, including the Gypsy mayor's son. The teachers and school principal were dancing with the girls so they wouldn't have to dance with the Gypsies. The mayor's son tried to cut in on the principal. The principal gave the Gypsy a dirty look and told him to go home and clean up if he wanted to dance with the girls. The Gypsy got mad and spat in his face. The principal simply caught his breath and remained calm, feeling thankful that nothing more happened. After a break, the Gypsy asked the principal's wife to dance. She agreed because she didn't want any more trouble. Had they tried to settle the score with the Gypsy, the principal would have been in trouble, no one else. These occurrences were hard to endure.

The Saxons worked hard all spring and summer on their farms, harder than usual, since there were so few of them left to work the land. At harvest time, the Gypsies and Romanians, who had lain in the shade all summer, came and took whatever they wanted. Saxons were lucky if they got to keep any of their hard-earned crops.

Rumors spread that the Romanian government was going to take all the Germans' houses. Rev. Herberth went to see the Bishop and learned that there was no law saying Saxons would have to give up their homes. When the time came for them to turn over their house keys, they refused. The officials were astounded, and sent some soldiers to take the houses, one by one. But every house was locked, so the soldiers returned to the courthouse. Rev. Herberth and two other men went to the courthouse and pleaded with the officials to let the people keep their homes. The Romanians responded by beating the minister, who cried out the window for help. Villagers ran in and fought against the officials and Gypsies who had come to get free houses. It didn't help; the officials hauled Rev. Herberth and the two other men off to jail in Hermannstadt (Sibiu).

They were held there for three months, until a large keg of wine convinced their jailers to open the doors. Bribery always greased the wheels in Romania.

Since the Romanians couldn't take the Saxons' houses, they moved Gypsy families into Saxon houses-two families in a single family home. Some of the Germans couldn't stand this forced quartering and left. There were not enough Gypsies in Reichesdorf to move into each home, so officials made plans to bring Gypsies in from other Romanian villages. When the German Reichesdorfers learned of this, they met the wagons at the edge of town and turned the Gypsies away.

The following week, the Romanians got organized: they grabbed Saxons off the streets and out of their homes and marched them to the courthouse. There were not a lot of Germans left who could fight them off. Many men were away in the army and the remaining able-bodied men and women had been taken to the Soviet labor camps. Only the old and very young were left. What a hopeless fate! When word got out of what was going on, people ran to the fields to escape.

Romanians beat the captured Saxons and threw them one by one into the basement of the courthouse, very injured and in pain. Margaret Zink's mother was grabbed by the hair and pulled down the stairs. One man died.

Later that evening, the captured men and women crawled or hobbled out of the basement, Father among them. Mother said that he came home moaning and groaning with broken ribs, the result of a particularly severe beating. He lay in bed for a long time while she nursed him back to health.

A Gypsy family took over our big kitchen. My parents had to build a kitchen for themselves at the back of the house. They left my sister Sinni at home during the day to watch them, and stop them from taking what little was left. She was still pretty young. Once, when one of the Gypsies was going to take something, she told him to leave it. He came after her. Frightened, she ran to Grandmother's house and slept under the bed there for several nights.

We stored grain in a locked bin in the shed. My family kept checking to make sure the lock was in place. However, when they needed some grain and opened the bin, it was nearly empty. The Gypsies had carved a hole in the back of the bin and siphoned off the grain.

Community Perseverance

Our church community had always encompassed the school and the community hall. The State took over the school and community hall, but fortunately left the church building and the minister's house alone. The State did take over the church's forested piece of land, however, its major source of income. This forced the Saxons to find another way to pay church taxes.

Transylvanian Saxons' last refuge was their Lutheran church, which, in spite of everything, persevered.

In 1947, the Romanians wanted to trade their little school for the much bigger German one. After much debate with the Saxons, the Romanians finally settled on taking over just two of the classrooms in the larger building. The Saxons used the other two rooms and the gymnasium, which was converted into two more classrooms. Three Saxon teachers taught the four classes for German children. One of them took the two oldest classes held in the gym. They had mostly only Romanian books to work with, and very few German. It was hard to keep order during recess, especially in the beginning. The Germans had to have a lot of patience and be careful not to offend the Romanians. A Romanian principal ran up to four inspections a week. The school always passed.

The Gypsies wanted to take the German school's musical instruments. The teacher made a deal: if the boys would come to school, he would teach them to play the instruments, but they wouldn't be allowed to take the instruments home. Also, the instruments could be used for State celebrations, as long as they were returned immediately.

Desperation

There was a lot of turnover in City Hall. No one wanted to stay because too many people were vying for the top position. The uneducated ones wanted to be the bosses. Village government grew more and more unstable.

A deranged Gypsy, who lived in the neighboring village Nimesch, thought he was the ruler of Europe. He terrorized a lot of boys by telling them he would shoot them. They became members of his gang to avoid being shot. The gang killed several people and stole from many more.

Reichesdorf was concerned that the same fate could befall them.

Reichesdorf's Romanian judge had a Gypsy living with him. The judge was butchering a pig one day, with a Saxon helping him. The Gypsy, in a rage, took an ax to the door. Both the Romanian and Saxon had to jump out a window to get away from him.

The Saxons worked what used to be their own land for a stipend, but the Gypsies and Romanians got all the harvest. The Gypsies thought they could live off the produce of the Saxon's hard work: meat, fruits, grain, wine, and other supplies. As time went on though, the reserves ran out. There were hardly any cows left amongst the Saxons. Many of the fields went unplanted, as there was no seed, and not enough people willing to work the land. Prices in the store climbed very high. As Gypsies led away the last cow, the Germans wondered how they would ever feed and clothe all the children who'd been left behind after the deportation. Things had to change.

A Small Break

Finally, about three years after the deportation, Soviets transported some of the weak and sick workers from the slave camps home to Romania. My cousin, Katharina Untch, was one of these. In time, the former slaves grew stronger and were able to help on the collective farms. Still, there was a shortage of food for the winter and, now, more mouths to feed. People who had a few extra potatoes or corn had already sold them in the fall for money. The deportees who lasted the whole five years laboring in the USSR, (such as my sister Yinni) came home to a very different world from the one they had left.

PART II
GERMANY

CHAPTER 8

Homeland

Leaving Ukraine

The Soviets gave me a coat, enough material for a skirt, and a pair of shoes. This was so I would look somewhat presentable when I left Ukraine. My cousin, Johanna (Untch) Nemenz had a needle and thread, and hand-stitched a skirt for me.

A couple of weeks after being marched naked before the Soviet commission, those of us who were selected as too weak to continue working were taken to the train. This train had bunk beds with straw. It was a relief to get out of there and we were glad to be heading home. The date is etched in my mind: April 9, 1947.

The Russian Zone

Twelve days later, on April 21, the train pulled into Frankfurt an der Oder, on the Poland/East Germany border. The Allied nations had divided Germany into four zones: the USSR controlled the east, Britain the northwest, America the south, and France the western edges. During the first two years of forced reparations and labor camps, the Soviets transported the sick and weak laborers to the Russian Zone, East Germany.

Officials took us to a camp, where we learned that, not only were they *not* going to take us to Romania; they weren't even going to *allow* us to go home. By this time, all my emotions had shut down. I couldn't feel anything. I couldn't laugh or cry. I was numb. It was all I could do just to put one foot in front of the other. I couldn't reason or make decisions. I couldn't go home and I didn't care.

Me after two years in the Soviet work camps
I re-made this sweater from a ratty, holey cardigan into a pull-over.

We stayed in the camp several weeks to get paperwork, and to have our clothes deloused one more time. Because we had learned German in school, we could understand the people there. They couldn't understand us, though, when we spoke Såksesch. They gave us shots for typhus and quarantined us for 14 days. Thankfully, I'd saved Kathi's card with her address. She lived in Delitzsch, 144 miles away. While in quarantine, I wrote to her.

Kathi traveled by train to be in Frankfurt an der Oder when they released us. I hadn't seen her for about a year and a half. She brought rolls saved from her own rations. This was so typical of her: always thinking of others. She knew some of the people who had been sent there with me and divided the bread amongst everyone. How I wanted all those rolls to myself!

The Soviets let me out of the camp on May 8, 1947 with a paper that showed I had served and been released from my obligation to the USSR.

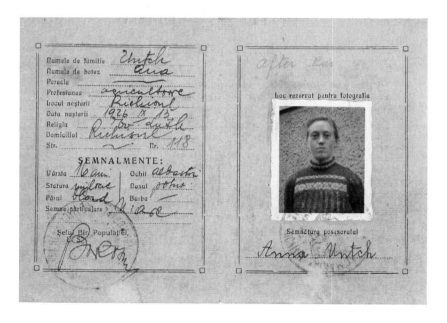

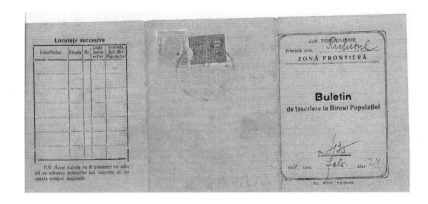

Travel Papers

While the other released workers were placed with farmers in the area, Kathi took me on a train to Delitzsch, into the center of the Russian Zone, to live with her. I don't remember a lot of what happened during this time because I was so out of it. She made all the decisions and arrangements for us. I couldn't even help.

On the three-hour trip to Delitzsch, the train stopped and we decided to get out and use a restroom. It was a nice, sunny day. I finished before Kathi and stood in the sunshine, waiting for her. Obviously I looked really bad because a woman came along and stuffed a sandwich into my hand, and then disappeared before I could thank her. I was so glad to have that sandwich!

Grateful, and yet embarrassed at the same time. Imagine seeing someone who looked so emaciated that you would give them your own lunch, at a time when there wasn't much food to go around! It was a good, tasty sandwich and I shared it with Kathi.

My sister shared two small rooms in the basement of a factory with eight other girls. We slept on a cement floor, using straw for a mattress. Both Kathi and I still had our blankets from home. I think we used the factory's kitchen, for the little cooking we did, as well as the restroom.

Kathi worked part time in a drugstore, filling bottles with cough syrup. She got a little money, but there was no food available to buy, except what could be purchased with our weekly ration cards.

Friends

I quickly found that East Germany had some very good people. Father's friend, Mischael Offner, who had also served in the Soviet labor camps, had been able to get into West Germany – the American Zone. There, he had met a nun, and they got to talking about her sister in Delitzsch.

Mr. Offner told the nun that his friend's daughter was living in Delitzsch, too. They had decided that the two should meet, so the nun wrote to her sister, Mrs. Kraft. Mr. and Mrs. Heinrich Kraft had then walked to the factory and introduced themselves to Kathi. They told Kathi about their two daughters: Susanna, who taught Kindergarten in Nurnberg, and Brigitte, in college.

Soon after we arrived in Delitzsch, Kathi and I walked to the Kraft's apartment so she could introduce me to them. Mr. Kraft stared at my very thick shoes, which the Soviets had given me. They looked too heavy for such a thin girl, so he weighed them. They were two pounds each! He couldn't believe I had the strength to lift my feet in them. The Krafts got me some used clothes from friends: a polka-dot shirt, a dark skirt, and black shoes. We were fortunate to have such wonderful friends and visited them often. They were very interested in what we'd been through and asked questions whenever we got together.

We learned that Mrs. Kraft used to ride her bicycle out to the fields to glean what had been left from harvest. But, the bicycle tires had worn out. We mentioned this in a letter to my Aunt

Anna and Uncle Hans Untch (Father's brother, Johann) in Prosser, Washington. After they'd received the letter, they sent us a package of food and clothes. In it there were two bicycle tires for Mrs. Kraft!

[Years later, Brigitte Kraft (now Muller) and her husband would visit us in Prosser. They borrowed our pickup and camper and traveled around the Northwest. I visited her home in Germany when I traveled to the area 30+ years later.]

Mr. and Mrs. Kraft

Surviving

A friend of the Krafts had an old parachute. They unraveled the silky strands of cord and gave me some. It was soft and fine and very durable. I used it to knit some underwear, camisoles, and socks for Kathi and myself. The clothing took a lot of time to finish, which kept me busy. There were no jobs available, so I had nothing but time on my hands. I still have the camisole of my set today.

The avenue that ran from Delitzsch to the factory was lined with pear trees. As the fruit ripened, a guard would walk back and forth to protect it. But, I *really* wanted that fruit! I kept thinking about our pears in Reichesdorf and how someone else would be stealing them. So one evening, when the guard turned to go the other way, I climbed up a tree, picked as many as I could carry, and slid back down before he saw me. When I stepped into the factory basement with the pears, my sister's eyes widened in disbelief. In my way of thinking, I wasn't stealing; I was just trying to survive. To a starving person, those pears were not only incredibly delicious, they were necessary!

As a girl, I'd had a dentist in Mediasch take care of my teeth and fill my cavities. But, after two and a half years in Ukraine without dental care or toothbrushes or proper nourishment, most of my teeth were beyond saving. So, while in East Germany, I had eleven teeth pulled. The dentist was very nice, and very sorry he had to pull so many.

Because of all the good people in my life at this time, I slowly came out of my numbness. Walking to church and worshiping every Sunday helped, too.

In Delitzsch, East Germany, befriended by the Krafts

Getting Out of East Germany

As soon as I had arrived in East Germany, Kathi and I wrote to Father that we were together in Delitzsch. For the next five months, he searched for a place for us to go. We wanted to go home to Romania, but he said there was no future for us there. Our friends in Delitzsch were very kind, good people, but not family. Family is the most important thing. Family is *everything*. So Father wrote to his brother, our Uncle Hans in Prosser, and asked if he would sponsor us to go to America. He and his wife, Aunt Anna, agreed, but we would need to get to the American Zone in West Germany, which would involve leaving the Russian Zone and crossing through the British Zone.

Of course, we didn't have passports to go to another zone. But, Father knew a man from Birthalm, Romania who was also stuck in East Germany. He couldn't return to his family, so Father bought new shoes for this man's children, and in return, the man agreed to take us to the border of the British Zone. Kathi acquired fake passports from some acquaintances, which would get us from the British Zone to the American Zone. Father's friend took us first by train, as far as it would go, and then walked with us through the forest toward the British Zone. He stopped just short of the border, where we could see it, and we went on alone. Finally, Kathi and I stepped out of the forest on the British side, into bright sunshine and the sound of church bells ringing. It was glorious. One border crossed and one more to get to the American Zone.

We walked to a little restaurant and ordered soup. It tasted so good, and we didn't need ration cards to buy it! At that point, we got a scare. A policeman came in and wanted to see our papers. Fortunately, he was satisfied with our fake passports and left us alone.

On the train ride across the border to the American Zone, another official asked our names and wanted to see our passports. I was terrified and had a hard time remembering the name on mine. It was obvious that the pictures on them weren't ours. He sent us back to the British Zone on the next train. We were very stupid to think the borrowed passports would get us across the border! But we did desperate things in those desperate times.

Back in the British Zone, we walked into a busy restaurant, which had only one empty chair left at a small table. I let Kathi have the chair and sat on the floor. She started talking to some people at the next table. One of them was a truck driver with a load for the American Zone. For a package of cigarettes, he agreed to hide us in the back of his truck. (Cigarettes were like gold. We could get them with our food stamps.) So, we rode like cargo across the border to the American Zone. Success!

The American Zone – West Germany

We traveled through West Germany to the home of Father's friend, Misch Offner in Weißenhorn, in the southern part of Germany. Within a couple of days, Misch had found us jobs and a place to stay. I worked in a greenhouse and Kathi worked as a housekeeper.

It didn't take long for us to connect up with other Reichesdorfers. Misch's daughter, Regina, lived in the area with her husband, a schoolteacher from Reichesdorf. She'd married him when she was fifteen. Margaret Waffenschmidt, who'd gone to school with Kathi and Regina, lived nearby as well. She had left Romania before the end of the war to visit her brother in Germany and consequently, had avoided the forced labor camps. Stephan Zink, her boyfriend, also lived near us. He was a Saxon, but from a different village in Romania.

In Augsburg with the Wagners

To get the paperwork required for us to stay in the American Zone, we had to go to a camp in Augsburg. Augsburg was quite some distance from our Reichesdorf friends: 57 miles away to the east. We stayed in the camp for two weeks. After giving us our papers, officials placed me with the Wagners, a family that owned a greenhouse in Augsburg. They placed Kathi with the Pfaff family – factory owners – to work as their maid. We worked for room and board and very little money. Sometimes we would get together on Sundays.

One Sunday, I went to the Lutheran church in Augsburg. The minister talked about his aunt in Romania and how little she had to eat. I started to cry. My tears flowed and my heart poured out. I felt better, but thought it was odd that no one said a word. A lot of displaced people from other countries lived there, and the locals didn't like being crowded in by so many foreigners. The war had left many homeless.

On Easter Sunday, the church overflowed with people. The pastor gave a long sermon and then served communion. This made me late getting back to the Wagners and Mrs. Wagner scolded me for taking so long. She thought I should have gotten up in the middle of the service and returned to her house in time to prepare the potato salad.

The Wagners raised vegetables. In early spring, we planted seeds in little boxes, and put them in the hothouse. Once the plants were two inches tall, we knelt on a plank and planted the seedlings in a hotbed. When the plants had grown to four inches, we transplanted them into the field. Mr. Wagner had overhead sprinklers to irrigate them.

Mrs. Wagner sold the vegetables in her produce stand. People traveled from town to buy from her. I remember American soldiers coming to purchase some.

Hired hands also came to help with the hothouse and garden. Once, when the day workers went home, I quit my greenhouse work too, and went into the house. Mrs. Wagner asked, "How come you quit?" Well, the other workers had quit. But, she told me, there was still plenty of work to do! Sometimes I chopped wood, sometimes swept up, and other times played with their eight- year-old daughter in the hay, even though it was really dusty. As long as I didn't go in the house, it was okay.

Mrs. Wagner had a pet dog. She would butter bread for the dog to eat, but because of rationing, there wasn't enough butter for my bread. I don't have good memories of living with Mrs. Wagner.

Connecting with Friends

Kathi and I tried to contact people we knew from Reichesdorf. All the Saxons in Germany were trying to reconnect with others from home. Most of our information came from our parents who heard about our friends from their parents. One day, seven *long* months after I'd arrived at the Wagners, Georg Binder, from Reichesdorf, knocked on the door. He had gone to school with Kathi. His sister, Regina, and I were friends from the labor camps. Georg lived in Goldach, 53 miles east of Augsburg, along with several others from Reichesdorf. He told me about the Fischers, an old couple in Goldach, who needed a maid. I was eager to leave the hard work of the greenhouse, and I certainly wouldn't miss the Wagners! So I went. Kathi, however, stayed in Augsburg.

In Goldach with the Fischers

I traveled to Goldach and moved in with the Fischers, a very nice older couple. The Fischers had a farm and a hired hand. Their married son was missing in action. His wife had her own place, but her daughter, the Fischers' granddaughter, lived with us. Little Maria was four or five years old and going to Kindergarten. She would ask me to comb her hair. Mrs. Fischer was always so afraid I wouldn't like the food she prepared. She didn't need to worry. I ate everything! For the first time in years, I got to eat as much as I wanted. Finally, I gained weight and got my strength back.

Even though I was hired as a maid, I mostly worked outside, farming. The Fischers grew hay, potatoes, and rhubarb; and raised pigs, cows, and horses. I pitched hay, harvested potatoes, cleaned the barns, and sometimes helped with the milking and feeding. One time I helped Mr. Fischer load the wagon with produce for the market in Munich. I tossed the heads of cabbage, maybe a little too hard, and he gave me a "watch out" look.

In West Germany, I had to have more dental work done. The dentist put crowns on my remaining teeth and made me stainless steel bridges for the missing ones. He was neither as kind nor as gentle as the East German dentist. The corners of my mouth hurt a lot after he worked on me.

Entertainment

The Reichesdorfers living in Goldach included Georg Binder and his sister, Regina, and their cousin Andreas Kloos. My second cousin Misch Greger was also in the area, as well as my second cousins, Regina and Johann Waffenschmidt. Johann (Hans) worked on a farm. All these young men had been in the German army and had the Waffen-SS tattoo on the inside of their left arms, just below their armpits. The tattoos identified their blood-types. All the women had served in the labor camps.

In Goldach, an organization held a dance every Saturday and all the local young Saxons from the Siebenburgen area of Romania would go. Even though some worked in neighboring towns, Goldach served as our weekend gathering spot. It was good entertainment and a good way for us to meet others. The hall had its dance floor upstairs. In front of a live band, we danced waltzes, polkas, and other steps. Downstairs, the hall had tables, where farmers gathered to drink beer.

Once, a group of us took a bicycle trip to Munich for Oktoberfest. We got up early and peddled for two or three hours, 18 miles southwest, in order to arrive in time to see the big parade. We made it and got to see troops of people from various parts of Germany parade by, each wearing the *trachten* (costumes) from their area of the country. Different bands marched by as well. The Oktoberfest also had a carnival, with all kinds of food, and of course, beer. A lot of people went to that Oktoberfest. In the afternoon, we biked back to Goldach, before it got dark.

Georg Binder

Georg Binder started showing more interest in me. I was a little surprised; he was my sister's age, so I figured they would pair up. His skills in carpentry eventually got him a job in Munich. He worked hard and earned enough money to buy land. Germany, however, was too crowded and land expensive and hard to come by. Georg was a good craftsman and kind of cute. He gave me a very nice wooden box that he'd made. Most importantly, though, he had a wonderful sense of humor and could dance really well! We talked about getting married, but he wanted to wait until he had land.

I wrote to Father about Georg. He told me that, before courting Mother, he had gone with Georg's mother for a little while, so he knew the family. Still, he told me to be careful.

The Season of Engagements

Meanwhile, Kathi had fallen for Peter Drotleff. Peter worked for the same farmer as Misch Offner. He was also from the Siebenburgen area, but not from Reichesdorf. Peter and Kathi got engaged.

Others among our friends became engaged. My sister and I went to the engagement party of Stephan Zink and Margaret Waffenschmidt. There were a lot of Saxons there, including Margaret's second cousin Misch Offner.

Tragedy

Father wrote to Kathi and me regularly. I looked forward to seeing his handwriting on the envelope because it meant news from home. In his businessman way, he told us about the farming, described the work they were doing, and told us they had enough to eat. He also kept us up on how the townspeople were, who had died, and so forth.

One day, I got a letter with Mother's handwriting instead, and knew immediately something was wrong. She told me Father and my brother Hans had come home one day with a wagonload of apples. A Gypsy woman followed them into the yard and told Father he didn't need to plow his field because it didn't belong to him anymore. He collapsed and had to be helped into the house. Mother said that the left side of his face wouldn't work and that he couldn't talk.

Several days later, Georg came over to tell me Father had died. In another few days, Mother's letter arrived telling me the same thing. Father had died October 8, 1949, about ten days after his stroke. His body was cold in his grave by the time her news reached me. He hadn't even reached 60. I cried for a week. I remember trying to pick apples and not being able to see through my tears. Mrs. Fischer expressed her concern and commented on how much I must have loved my father. There was no way for me or Kathi to get back to Romania. I felt so isolated and helpless. The last time I had seen Father was in Mediasch, when he brought us warm clothes before we were shipped to Ukraine. Now, I would never see him again. I was miserably broken hearted.

Peter and Kathi (left) with Friends in West Germany
The woman with her two daughters was a German teacher from Romania

Getting Papers

All of us with relatives in America were trying to get sponsored. We started the paperwork to go to the U.S. about the same time. The officials required us to have all sorts of medical checkups before we could be cleared to go to America. Uncle Hans in Prosser also worked on papers for us at his end. He didn't have a lot of land and so didn't appear to have enough wealth to sponsor anyone. So, he wrote in prominent Prosser names on the papers to add influence.

Back in Romania – My Changing Family
Yinni has returned from work camp Father has died
Hans is around 17 and Sinni about 12

It took two and a half years from when we arrived in Germany before the first ones in our group were able to leave. It took much longer for the men to be approved because they had served in the German Army. This became an insurmountable difficulty for some of the romances.

Stephan Zink had a farmer in Vernon, BC sponsor him. He told his minister in Vernon that he and his fiancé *had* to get married, which raised some eyebrows. He went to Vernon, BC then sent for Margaret. Margaret took a ship across the Atlantic, then the train across North America. When she got to the seemingly endless prairies, she was about to turn around. It was just so desolate. She was pretty pleased with the hills and mountains around Vernon, BC. Margaret didn't have any place to stay long term, hence the need to get married right away. Soon after she arrived, the minister married them. That's how Stephan and Margaret Zink ended up in Canada.

Before Kathi and I left for America, Georg gave me a ring. We celebrated the engagement at the dance hall.

PART III
AMERICA

United States

CHAPTER 9

A Foreigner Again

S. S. Volendam, From Holland to New York

The Journey

In February 1950, my second cousin Regina Waffenschmidt and my friend Regina Binder, Georg's sister, left Germany for relatives in New York. The next month, Kathi and I got our papers and left Germany by train for Rotterdam, Holland. There, we boarded the former war ship, Volendam, and set sail for New York, via Halifax, Canada. There were a lot of Dutch people on the ship, headed for Canada. We traveled in third class and slept on bunk beds, again. Everywhere we went there were bunk beds! At least these ones had mattresses. (The people in first class had much nicer accommodations.) I was very seasick for all 13 days of the trip, and didn't eat much. Kathi brought me bread crusts. Unknown to me, she didn't feel well either, but for a different reason.

The American officials didn't process us at Ellis Island; it was being renovated. Instead, before we docked, they came out on a small boat, climbed onto the *Volendam*, and checked our paperwork.

Finally, in April 1950, the ship docked and we walked down the plank onto the New York pier. There, we saw a most wonderful thing: Regina Waffenschmidt, her aunt and uncle, Regina Binder, and her aunt and uncle were all waiting there to meet us, waving in greeting! We were *so* happy to see them, and to finally be in America! By this time, we felt closer to these friends than our own family members, because we had lived and suffered together in Ukraine.

The Waffenschmidts took us to their home to rest and get over our seasickness. Then, they entertained us, taking us sightseeing and to a play.

Three days after we had arrived, our hosts took Kathi and me to the airport. After all we'd been through, the flight to Seattle didn't scare us. The old, noisy plane took off and landed several times along the way across the country. Flight attendants kept coming around, asking us in English – which we didn't understand – what we wanted to drink. They offered to let us get off and stretch at the stopovers, but we didn't understand and we were *not* about to leave that plane!

At the Seattle airport, some strangers came up to us and handed us a letter from our uncle. In it, Uncle Hans told us that these people meeting us, Bill and Evelyn Pittman, were friends of his and Aunt Anna's. He wanted us to go with them; they would take us to Prosser. So, we went with the Pittmans to their house. We couldn't speak to each other, but we used lots of gestures. Evelyn took us by the hands and showed us where the beds were. Kathi and I lay down and rested while Bill fixed dinner.

In the morning, we saw that the table was set again, so we sat down and ate. Then, they motioned us to the car. It was a nice car and we had a comfortable ride to Prosser.

First thing upon our arrival, Aunt Anna and Uncle Hans had to check us out: see what we looked like and how much we'd grown, and examine our health after the years of starvation and hard labor. Aunt Anna hadn't seen us since we were little, when she visited Reichesdorf, and Uncle Hans had never seen us. Finally, we had someone we could speak with! We talked and laughed about all the sign language we'd had to use since arriving in the U.S. Uncle Hans ("Uncle Jack" now that we were in America) was a wonderful guy, quite tall and slim. He had a great sense of humor and really liked to joke around. He called Aunt Anna "Shorty," which truly fit, especially when she stood next to him.

We all ate dinner and then the Pittmans went to the Prosser Motel. The closet in the bedroom Kathi and I shared held a suit and a nice dress for each of us.

Aunt Anna, Kathi, Me, and Uncle Jack

Adapting

As happy as we were to be in Prosser, it took a while to get used to the barren, treeless hills around us. Our childhood had been filled with lush, green, tree-covered hills.

We also struggled with the language barrier. Just about everyone in Prosser knew that my uncle had been working for two years on our immigration papers, with the help of attorney H. N. Nelson. Many people wanted to talk to us and to hear our story. It was difficult because Aunt Anna and Uncle Jack had to interpret. People were very friendly. Thankfully, no one thought of us as "Nazis." Everywhere we went, they asked us to sing.

The people in Prosser pronounced our names differently. I was no longer *"Ahh-na"* but *"Ann-a,"* and Kathi was no longer *"Kaugh-ty"* but *"Kay-ty."*

We kept busy, crocheting and trying to learn English. Kathi helped around the house and I helped Uncle Jack put in fence posts.

I kept asking if the postholes were deep enough. Is that enough? Deep enough? Uncle Jack started calling me "Enough."

Pregnant

Kathi and I were lying in bed one night, talking, and she told me she was pregnant. I started to shake and couldn't breathe. Here we were in a strange land, surrounded mostly by strangers, and my sister was in a *very* disgraceful situation. Kathi was utterly ashamed. She said, "How could this have happened to *me*? *Of all people?* And at *my* age?" Of course she had known better, but war had changed everything. In Germany there had been a "live for today" feeling because, after all we'd been through and might continue to go through, we couldn't be sure of our futures.

As her stomach grew bigger, Kathi hid whenever people came to the door, not wanting them to see her unwed and pregnant. Aunt Anna thought she was bloated from starvation. It was her friend, Christina Wilson, who knew right away and told her, "That girl is pregnant." Aunt Anna had never had children and, fortunately for us, was eager to have a baby in the house.

The Best Parents

Uncle Jack was Father's oldest brother. He had immigrated to Ohio as a young man, where he met and married Anna Waffenschmidt (also from Reichesdorf.) He worked there in a factory, making gadgets. Then, he and Aunt Anna moved to Seattle and sold produce at Pike Place Market. After that, they moved to Prosser and raised chickens and turkeys.

Kathi and me feeding Uncle Jack's chickens

Aunt Anna & Uncle Jack were very good to us, like the best parents anyone could ever have had. When Kathi and I spoke in Såksesch to each other, Uncle Jack would holler, "You're in America now! You speak like an American!" He was not strict like his businessman brother, Simon, though. Where Father had worked all the time, Uncle Jack knew how to live, how to have fun.

He was like a kid. Aunt Anna and Uncle Jack were always okay with whatever I did.

Uncle Jack loved to go to farm auction sales, and he liked having someone go with him. He would ask me, "Well, Slim Jim, do you want to go with me to the sale?" I enjoyed getting out, and I liked the action and how fast the auctioneers talked. Uncle Jack warned me not to scratch my nose, or I might end up buying something! Once, he pointed out a bicycle. I got it for six dollars and was pretty happy, even if it was a boy's bike. Then, I bought some new tires for it. After taking a couple of spills, I learned to not take corners too fast in gravel.

Me
(Uncle Jack and Kathi in back)

More Dental Work

I had to see a dentist, again. This one was so shocked at the bridge the German dentist had put in my mouth that he called his associate to come look at it. Apparently, they'd never seen a bridge made from stainless steel before!

As it turned out, I would have all my teeth pulled when I was 36. I had dentures the rest of my life.

Neighbors and New Friends

Uncle Jack knew some German people in town who had a sewing machine business. Their nephew had arrived seven months before from Poland. He spoke German, but could already get by in English. He took Kathi and me places once in a while, including the Buena Vista Grange Hall dedication. He loaned us a book on how English was spelled and pronounced. It helped a lot. Later, I bought my first piece of furniture from them – a cabinet with a sewing machine on top that could fold down and tuck inside.

All the farmers in our neighborhood would help each other out from time to time. The closest neighbor, Alfred Melgaard across the road, raised dairy cows. Not long after we'd arrived in Prosser, he was going to need help chasing his calves across the road to different pasture. Uncle Jack taught me my first English sentence and sent me over to ask Alfred, "Are you ready with your calves?" It was a very long sentence for me. I found Alfred in his barn, washing his milking machines. I asked my question and waited for a simple "Yes" or "No." Instead, he rattled on and on, as if I could understand English! Finally, I turned around and left. The answer was obviously "No."

Alfred Melgaard on his dairy farm

The Schultzs needed help hoeing weeds in their vineyard, so we went over. Others had gathered there to help, too. It was a nice place and the Schultzs treated us well. Mrs. Schultz thought Kathi and I needed an outing, so she talked her son and his friend Paul

Larson, who was working there too, into taking us to a movie. I had never been to a movie in the States before. We could hardly communicate with the boys, but we had a good time. Mrs. Schultz was pleased with the results of her efforts.

The Wilsons

Mr. and Mrs. Victor Wilson, living on Brown Street in Prosser, were friends and former neighbors of our aunt and uncle. They visited us almost every weekend and sometimes during the week to help with butchering chickens or whatever came up. Mrs. Wilson, Christine, babysat a lot and was always kissing babies. People would say, "She'll come slobber up my children before I even get to meet them!" Everyone called them "Grandma" and "Grandpa" because they loved children so much.

The Wilsons took a special interest in Kathi and me. They had farmed in the White Bluffs area, but during the formation of the Hanford Nuclear Reservation, all the residents were forced to leave. So the Wilsons felt like they had a lot in common with us because we had both lost our homes. Also, they'd never had any children of their own, but they had adopted Christina's sister's son, Clyde. The sister had been unwed and too young to raise the child. Victor and Christine were very understanding people.

Mr. Wilson was always ready to listen, teach and talk. He had a lot of patience. Politically, he liked the democrats, because they were generous. He had a wonderful sense of humor and wrote some great letters. We got to be quite close to the Wilsons. They became like parents to me, especially.

Victor and Christine on their 50th Wedding Anniversary

To Work

Uncle Jack talked to someone he knew at Prosser Pack and they hired Kathi and me during asparagus harvest. For two weeks, we took asparagus out of boxes and lined it up on a belt so that a machine could cut it. They gave us a nice paycheck. We were finally working for real money! This was important because we wanted to pay Uncle Jack and Aunt Anna back for all the money they'd spent on legal fees and travel tickets to get us to Prosser.

Kathi took on a few house cleaning jobs, too. She cleaned for the Mercers and for a family from the Lutheran church. During the summer potato harvest, I sorted potatoes at Copeland's Warehouse. Mrs. Backus, a friend who lived close by, drove me to work in her old car. The potatoes were on a moving belt and, for a while, the belt gave me motion sickness. I brought my lunch home uneaten, making Aunt Anna very worried about me.

Grape harvest came next. I loved to pick grapes because I came from grape country. My hands would fly! Several neighbors asked me to pick for them because I picked faster than anyone else. In one vineyard, Mrs. Backus took a row, I another row, and the two Guy brothers another. I passed them all! John Guy couldn't believe how fast I could pick, and came over to watch me.

Picking grapes made me feel like I was at home. I hadn't been the fastest in Reichesdorf, because I was just a kid then and goofed around a little too much. But, since arriving in America, I wanted to buy a car. I earned good money picking grapes and my savings grew.

Becoming an Aunt

Kathi's labor contractions started toward the end of the grape harvest. I had to go to work, so I told her goodbye and to bring home something nice.

When I got back that night, I heard she'd had a girl. The Lutheran minister and his wife drove into the yard, so I cleaned up in a hurry and rode with them to the hospital. Kathi looked pretty tired. Her baby was in the nursery. We talked about names. The minister's wife suggested

Elizabeth, after her. "Then you could call her Betty." But Kathi wanted a German name. My aunt suggested Anna, after her. Kathi finally settled on the name Anna. Aunt Anna said that since we had arrived in May that "May" could be her middle name. Actually, we had gotten there in April, but we liked the name Anna May.

Making Silage

Alfred Melgaard bought some field corn from Mrs. Backus and needed help making it into silage for his cows. The Backus boys chopped down the stalks, and Alfred hauled them in his trailer to the base of his silo. There, we put the leaves, ears, and stalks into the chopper, which ground them and blew the particles up into the 33-foot tall silo. Uncle Jack, inside the silo, spread and stomped on the silage to pack it down. At noon, Lucille Towne, Alfred's sister, brought a dinner of meatloaf and scalloped potatoes out for us. It tasted so good! In those days, people fed their help. Now workers have to bring a lunch.

Driving Lessons

Mr. Wilson cleaned and took care of the Grange Hall. He would pick me up on his way to work in his funny old car with running boards, and let me practice driving. In return, I would help him clean the Grange Hall. He had a lot of time on his hands, so he got the driver's manual and helped me study. When I could drive well enough, he let me drive all the way to Grandview! I told him I couldn't understand why they didn't make the roads wider. He really got a kick out of that. With his help, I studied hard and passed the written test. Then, I took the driving test and – just like the written one – passed the first time! After that, Jerry Johnson sold me a raffle ticket for a car. Oh, how I wanted that car! Someone else won it, but from then on, I had the fever.

A Nanny for the Johnsons

In October 1950, six months after we'd arrived, Jerry Johnson asked my aunt and uncle if he could hire me as a nanny and housekeeper. He needed someone to watch his boys so his wife could work in their store – "Jerry's" – in town. They sold men's clothing and did dry cleaning. Their oldest son, Dan, was seven and little Barry, two. The

Johnsons gave me a downstairs room in their house, and I watched the boys, cleaned house, did laundry, and cooked. They paid me $90 a month plus room and board. I learned a lot there: to cook, bake, and speak English. Sometimes, I would call them at the store if I had a question. I wasn't used to using the phone, and felt nervous because I still didn't know the language well and couldn't use my hands to help make myself understood. I talked so loud into the phone, they couldn't understand me. When they said they couldn't understand me, I talked even louder. Later, at home, they laughed and explained that you could talk in a normal voice into the phone.

Once, I raked leaves into a pile and burned them right there on the lawn. The neighbor called the Johnsons and told them I was burning their lawn. They just laughed and never got mad. I think Mrs. Johnson planted tulips in the burned spot. She kept asking Mr. Johnson to cut the hedge, but he never got around to it. One day, I took the pruners and cut the hedge myself. Mr. Johnson was so happy. His wife still thought he should have done it. She was patient, kind and helped me a lot. It was a good place to live.

On Sundays, the Johnsons would drop me off at the Lutheran Church and then take their family to the Presbyterian Church. One Sunday, Mrs. Johnson asked me why I didn't just go with them. So I did, and found I liked it better! That's how I got started worshiping at the First Presbyterian Church in Prosser.

After a year with the Johnsons, in the fall of 1951, Mrs. Frye told my aunt about a job opening at the Keen-Riverview School cafeteria. Aunt Anna and I both thought I should take it. After accepting the position, I was struggling with how to break the news to the Johnsons because they were so nice to me. Finally, I worked up the nerve to tell her after church. She was really hurt, in part because she had already heard about my leaving from Mrs. Krump, the head cook. I still worked for the Johnsons on weekends, cleaning and babysitting. Sometimes I was so tired I would fall asleep before they returned, and they had a tough time waking me to open the door for them.

Mrs. Gertrude Kilkinney

I moved out of the Johnsons' home and into a room in Mrs. Gertrude Kilkinney's house, near the school. She was in her forties and had been widowed as a young wife and mother, when her daughter was just a little girl. The daughter was now away at college. Mrs. Kilkinney worked as a cook in a restaurant. I would rake leaves or find other yard work to help her, and she would wash my uniform. I usually ate at the school cafeteria. Sometimes, we went to the movies together. On weekends, I rode my bike out to visit my aunt and uncle. That Halloween, Mrs. Kilkinney and I, two wild women looking for excitement, went out to Alfred's to trick-or-treat. At first, he didn't know who we were or what to make of the situation. But when he caught on, he really got a kick out of it. He asked us in and gave us some candy.

We played a card game before going home.

First Car

Mr. Wilson helped make my dream come true. When I finally had enough money saved up, he came with me to a car lot in town. He dealt with the salesman, and I was able to buy a three- year-old Kaiser for $600. It was a 1948 model, gray with four doors, and had fancy push-button, interior door openers. After that, I sold my bicycle for $10 – a $4 profit!

Uncle Jack, Aunt Anna, Me, Kathi, Anna May, and Peter Drotleff
At Anna May's Baptism

Peter Drotleff

Katharina wrote to her fiancé, Peter, constantly. Because he had served in the German army, it took him a lot longer to get paperwork processed to move to America. This made Katharina so angry. We'd been in Prosser nearly two years before he could get here. His baby girl had passed her first birthday. When he finally did arrive, he and Kathi went right away to the Prosser Court House and got married. Aunt Anna had a little get-together with a few friends afterward to celebrate.

Peter and Kathi – now Drotleff – stayed with Aunt Anna and Uncle Jack for a few months then took a one-bedroom apartment in town. I moved in with them to help pay the rent, and slept in the living room on a recovered hide-a-bed I'd bought in a second-hand store for $65. Peter worked odd jobs for farmer friends of Aunt Anna and Uncle Jack. Kathi cleaned a few houses.

In 1952, Aunt Anna and Uncle Jack decided to move to California. For one reason, Aunt Anna had terrible asthma in Prosser. Peter and Kathi chose to go with them. Kathi was eager to go, but I had a good job and so stayed and moved back in with Mrs. Kilkinney. I gave the hide-a-bed to some people from church, but left my aunt's armoire in the apartment for a while. Later, when I came to get it, the landlord wouldn't give it back. He kept it to "cover the cost of storage."

I didn't feel alone in Prosser after Kathi, Peter, Aunt Anna, and Uncle Jack moved. The Wilsons and Mrs. Kilkinney had become like family to me.

First Date

On his 47th birthday, April 10, 1952, Alfred Melgaard called, probably from the Grange Hall, and asked me to go *ins Kino* (to the movies.) He asked in German so no one around him would understand what he was doing. To avoid running into people who knew him, he took me to the drive-in theater in Sunnyside. After the movie, he said, "If you would leave George, I'd marry you." I told him I would think about it.

I thought for a long time, trying to decide what to do. I had promised to marry "George" (Georg) and had waited two years for him to come to Prosser. Because it was taking so long for him to get approval to immigrate to the United States, he'd gone to Venezuela, thinking he could get his papers faster from there. He couldn't, so he suggested I move to Venezuela. But, I had a job and family here. I had already learned English and didn't want to start over with another language.

The only person I knew in Venezuela was him, and he was a smoker and drank a lot. I hadn't been brought up with either of those things and didn't like them.

Alfred, on the other hand, was just the sort of man I wanted to marry. He was a farmer, a good Christian, very devoted to his church, and he didn't drink or smoke. He was fun, with a good sense of humor, but a hard worker. He didn't dance much, but he had a beautiful tenor voice and sang in the church choir. Father would have thought he was too old for me, but they would have enjoyed talking to each other. Both of them were talkers. Uncle Jack and Aunt Anna really liked Alfred, though, and were fine with the idea of us getting married.

Finally, I wrote Georg and told him that I had found someone else. He wrote a *very* angry letter in return and asked for his ring back. The letter was so awful I didn't want anyone to see it, so I burned it. I was glad, then, that I had *not* gotten him to America. I sent the ring back to him along with the wooden jewelry box he had made. That was the last I heard from him.

Alfred Eugene Melgaard at about 20
April 10, 1905 – March 26, 1985

Alfred Eugene Melgaard

Alfred's ancestors came from Norway. His father, *Alfred Andrew Melgaard*, had been only a baby when his parents emigrated – around 1868. They settled in Aberdeen, South Dakota and now, there are a *lot* of Melgaards in South Dakota! Alfred Andrew's father, *Andrew Melgaard*, gave Aberdeen 25 acres of land for a park. The city put a statue of him there in Melgaard Park.

"This Statue Erected in Memory of Andrew Melgaard, Pioneer, Who Presented this Park to the City of Aberdeen" (Unveiled in 1931)
http://www.aberdeenareahistory.org/items/show/238

Victor, Lucille, and Alfred Melgaard circa 1910

Alfred Eugene joined the family in Spokane which by then included a sister, Lucille. Their father, *Alfred Andrew Melgaard,* born in 1868, worked as a pharmacist there and their mother, *Jesse Horning Melgaard,* born Oct. 17, 1878, worked as a school teacher. Victor was born in the next city they lived in.

In 1919, when Alfred Eugene was 14, the family moved to Prosser. For $1,725 his father bought 9.2 acres, which included an apple orchard and a one-bedroom house, built in the late 1800's. He worked as a pharmacist in Prosser as well as substituted for pharmacists all up and down the valley. He never made any money, though; times were very tough. He raised apples, but the price for them was very low. When he took them to a warehouse, instead of giving him money, they billed him for the storage and sorting work!

Victor and Alfred Melgaard

Alfred's mother retired from teaching when she had Lucille. She taught Sunday School in Prosser, however. Alfred built up a dairy farm on the family property. During the Great Depression, he traded his dairy cream at the store for groceries. Lucille grew up to be a beautician and Victor went to Portland to be a dentist. During WWII, Victor worked as a dentist for the Navy.

Their father died in 1937 at the age of 69, leaving Jesse a widow for 15 years. Alfred took care of her in their family home when she grew sick with emphysema. Victor made sure she had things, like a toilet so she wouldn't have to go outside to the outhouse. He bought all the fixtures and then Alfred built a little bathroom off the porch.

When Kathi and I came over from Germany to Aunt Anna and Uncle Jack's, Jesse said to Alfred, "Wouldn't it be funny if you ended up with one of those Untch girls across the street?" She died on September 7, 1950, only a few months later. I didn't get to know her.

Courting

After his proposal in April of 1952, Alfred and I took the following year and nine months to get to know each other. Uncle Jack was disgusted that he kept our courtship hidden. Alfred's secrecy hurt my feelings a couple of times, but mostly, I understood. He'd had a reputation as a confirmed bachelor for so long, and had been a tremendous teaser with his buddies at the Grange when they had married. He knew they would retaliate in a big way if they knew he was seeing me. And, of course, our age difference would have made people talk.

During this time, I never passed up an opportunity to work. If there was harvesting, cleaning, babysitting, or painting to be done, I was there. One summer, I even painted the school cafeteria. The custodians joked that they would turn me in for painting without a license. Ever since I'd sat around, unemployed in East Germany, I was glad whenever I had something to do.

Road Trip

The summer of 1953, Mr. Wilson said, "I want to go and see Annie Untch, even if I have to take the bus." Mrs. Wilson had a sister in San Diego and offered to pay for gas if I would drive Mr. Wilson and her and her other sister, Kate, in my car. The two sisters baked and cooked ahead of time so there would be plenty to eat on the trip. I wanted Alfred to go along so we could get married in California, but he was too busy with the farm.

We got up really, really early and Mr. Wilson drove until traffic picked up. I watched for signs. The speed limit then was 50 miles per hour. When I drove, Mr. Wilson watched for signs. He was good at that. We would drive about 500 miles a day and then try to get a room fairly early. Because of Mrs. Wilson and Kate's packed food, we didn't have to spend money on meals.

One day, we were going down a big hill when my brakes gave out. I struggled with the steering wheel while Mrs. Wilson and Kate prayed in the back seat. The prayers were answered; we survived! We had to interrupt the road trip to get new brakes for my car, though.

Everyone was happy when we got to La Mesa, California in one piece – both the California group and the ones in the car. After a good visit, the Wilsons continued on to San Diego to see Mrs. Wilson and Kate's sister. Mr. Wilson had my car serviced there. I stayed with Aunt Anna and Uncle Jack, Kathi, Peter, and little Anna May, who was now two and a half years old. The two families didn't live very far apart. Through the minister of their church, Peter had gotten a good job as a janitor for the gas and electric company. Kathi cleaned houses.

While we were there, we went to Mexico for a day. Uncle Jack drove his car to Tijuana. At the border, he told them he was from Ohio! (Well, technically he was: he'd lived in Ohio when he first immigrated to America.) We went to the open air market where I bought some shoes and a leather purse. I also ended up with a ceramic bank in the shape of a bull because the guy kept running after me, pestering me to buy it. We got our picture taken in front of a cart with a donkey, wearing big sombreros. At the end of the day, we drove back to La Mesa.

In Mexico with a painted donkey!
Aunt Anna, Kathi and Anna May, Me, and the "Driver"

We went to Balboa Park a couple of times, where Aunt Anna bought Anna May rides on the amusements. At the zoo, we watched some animal tricks and visited the petting area. The monkeys were fun, swinging around or picking bugs off each other. There were flamingos standing in a pond. We ate at a restaurant there. Everyone had a good time.

The Wilsons, Kate, and I took the scenic route on the way back from California. We stopped in Stockton for two nights to visit Kate's son. Then, we traveled through the Redwood Forest. The trees were huge! I drove my car on a road that went *through* one of them. Another one had a shop in the base of its trunk.

Me with my Kaiser inside a redwood tree

Victor Wilson in front of the redwood tree store

In Crescent City, we spent a night and visited the Wilson's adopted son, Clyde. He had married and had a son, Walter. Clyde and his wife were good parents and raised a good family.

From there, we drove all the way back to Prosser. I was quite eager to be home and it obviously showed. A policeman pulled me over and I asked him, "Oh, was I going too fast?" From the back seat, Kate said, "Yes you were." I got off with a warning.

Getting Married

At the end of the summer, I started cooking at school again. Alfred didn't have time to get married until after he finished putting up silage. Finally, later that fall, we went to get the marriage license - in Ellensburg so no one in Prosser would read about it in the paper. Mrs. Wilson, always eager to go for a ride, came along as a witness.

I had been trying to keep quiet about all the wedding preparations, but my secretiveness stirred up Mrs. Kilkinney's curiosity. So two weeks before the big day, I stayed with the Wilsons. On the morning of December 18, 1953, Alfred came and picked me up. He had hired someone to watch the farm and the Backus boys to milk the cows. We picked up his sister, Lucille, on the way to Everett, where their brother, Victor, lived. Victor's wife, Donna, had the table set nicely.

Donna's mother, Mrs. Mosier, kept the food warm while we drove to Seattle for the wedding. The Melgaards had arranged for their friend, Rev. Dr. Jamison, to perform the ceremony in his home. Mrs. Jamison played the piano. The ceremony took half an hour. Then, we drove back to Vic and Donna's. On the way, we were pulled over because Vic had been speeding. He got out of the car and went back to talk to the officer. I'm not sure how it turned out.

Wedding Day December 18, 1953

We had a beautiful dinner at the Melgaard's. Afterward, Alfred and I spent the night in a hotel in Everett. The next morning, we went to Vic and Donna's for breakfast before Alfred, Lucille, and I returned to Prosser. On the way home, Alfred said he thought we should spend another night in a hotel. He was worried that his friends would pull something if they knew he had finally gotten married at the ripe old age of 48. Lucille made fun of him and said no one would bother us.

By the time we got back, the cows were all milked, but Alfred still had to prepare for his Sunday School lesson. I went to bed.

The Buena Vista Grange members, who had attended their annual dinner for the Carnation Company earlier that evening, just up the road from our house, kept driving by the house, waiting for the lights to go out. When Alfred finally came to bed, he heard a noise. "They're here!" he said. I told him not to worry, the door was locked. Alfred jumped into his overalls anyway.

Sure enough, Harry Palmer crawled in through our bedroom window and ran through the house to unlock the front door. I was so tired, but I got up and put on a robe. Thirty-five people spilled in through the front door! Everyone wanted to see my ring, and of course, everyone had to tease Alfred. They had planned for the jailor, Don Brown, to lock Alfred up for the night. Don had a jail cell waiting for him. Mr. Copeland, however, felt sorry for me, and talked them out of arresting him. Alfred promised them all chocolate bars and cigars.

The Travaille Family was there along with their teenage son Leonard. Decades later, he still remembered the excitement of the evening.

Finally, about one-thirty in the morning, the shivaree broke up, leaving us only a few hours to sleep before Alfred had to milk the cows. We couldn't crawl under the covers right away, however; there were nails in our bed.

In the morning, Alfred couldn't find his shoes; they were in the oven.

1956 Old Melgaard House – Ready to be moved

CHAPTER 10

Farming in the New Country

At church that first morning back in Prosser, after the sermon, Rev. Osterhoff announced that we had gotten married. No more secret; everyone knew. Alfred told people that I'd trapped him. He'd ridden in my car with its fancy push-button door openers and couldn't figure out how to get out of it.

Alfred didn't want me to work in the cafeteria anymore after that; he wanted me to stay home and tend to his "*calf*-eteria." This suited me. Of all the places I've lived and worked, farm life has always been my favorite: gardening, tending animals, and producing food. I had been very anxious to move onto the farm and fix it up.

Alfred had nine acres with the house and 20 more across Old Inland Empire Highway, which he had purchased earlier and paid off by 1948. He'd left that piece of land in pasture. I learned to drive the tractor and we plowed and disked his land across the road, then planted corn and cultivated. Now we had pasture and a corn field! He had a lousy old corn chopper, though, that required a *lot* of patching.

I wanted a nice-looking house, but the little Melgaard home had never been painted in its 60 plus years. Alfred had bought paint, but he hadn't gotten around to applying it. And now, he was too busy planting corn. So, I got to work. First, I scrubbed the outside with a wire brush, then painted the whole thing by myself – white with green trim. I stained the roof green, too!

The little house had no wasted space. When someone walked in from the wooden front porch, they stepped right into the living room. The bedroom was to the left and the kitchen straight ahead. The tiny bathroom, on the left side of the porch, had a toilet, a small shower, and a small sink. Up in the attic, bees built a hive one summer. But, they moved. I would have liked to have had some fresh honey, but no such luck.

We heated the house with an old oil stove and a trash burner. For appliances, we had a range and a refrigerator. The floors were covered with floral patterned linoleum. A telephone hung on the wall, connected to a party line, which included the Grange Hall and several neighbors. You couldn't make a call until everyone was off the line. But, you could listen in on other people's conversations. That's how you learned what was going on in the neighborhood. The number back then was Yukon 5-2893 or 985-2893.

1954, Californians Visit
On the porch of the Wilsons house Alfred, Me, Victor Wilson
Kathi, Christine Wilson, Anna May

Off the Farm

Alfred and I were active members of the Buena Vista Grange (an agriculture advocacy, support, and charitable fraternal society) on Old Inland Empire Highway, where Alfred served a term as Master. We were members of First Presbyterian Church on the corner of Yakima and Market.

Alfred served many terms there as a Church Elder, the last one being on the Finance Committee. He also taught Sunday School, was the Sunday School Superintendent, and sang in the church choir. I taught Sunday School for a little while as well. Alfred and I liked to sing together. From time-to-time, people would ask us to sing for events, like church worship services and Grange installation ceremonies.

Alfred served on the ASCS (Agricultural Stabilization and Conservation Service) for close to 20 years. As a part of this federal agency, he advised farmers on how to rotate their crops and how to reduce erosion. He also served on the FHA, (Farmers' Home Administration) a committee that assessed farms for loan worth. Taking on the role of "Water Master" of Sunnyside Valley Irrigation District, he cleaned out irrigation ditches and pipes in the spring, before the irrigation water was turned on.

Melgaard On FHA Board

PROSSER—Appointment of Alfred E. Melgaard as a member of the Benton County Farmers Home Administration Committee has been announced by Charles C. Wilson, county supervisor.

Melgaard owns and operates a dairy farm at Route 1, Prosser. He has been a resident of this area for a number of years and is active in community affairs. He is married and has one son and one daughter.

Three-Man Group

Two other members make up the three member committee which works with the county supervisor. Objectives are to provide the best possible use for the agency's farm credit service program consistent with local farmers' needs. Committee members are Sam S. Mecham, Benton City and Frank Lampson, Kennewick. Meacham will serve as chairman during the 1961 fiscal year.

Each member is appointed for three years. Melgaard succeeds William Pickard whose term expired this year.

Advance Credit

The Farmers' Home Administration makes annual or intermediate term loans to farmers who need adequate funds to buy equipment and livestock and longer term loans to build or repair houses and other essential farm buildings and to purchase or improve land suitable for family type farm operations.

It also advances credit to farmers or their non-profit associations to establish and carry out approved soil and water conservation practices and to install and improve irrigation and farmstead water facilities.

On the Farm

I wasn't much of a joiner. The farm, house, garden, and eventually children kept me busy enough. I would also help the neighbors on their farms as they needed. My garden produced flowers, vegetables, and fruit. I canned, preserved, or froze my crops. I baked – up to eight loaves of bread every week – and lots and lots of pies – especially apple. I also made our cheese and butter with the milk from our dairy. . The children said they loved coming home from school when I had made donuts (about 80-100) and smelling them before even opening the door. And everyone loved my cinnamon twists.

In the 1970s someone gave me some green bean seeds from the WSU Experiment Station. They were bush beans, delicious and they produced all summer. I planted a lot more after that and sold them to the grocery store. The children would pick beans and make a little money for themselves. I didn't mind the extra work, especially if you started before it got too hot.

We had up to 98 head of cattle at one time, including cows, steers, and calves. 42 of them were milking cows.

A Growing Family Needs a Bigger House

Lucille advised me, "If kids don't come, don't wait too long to adopt." Fortunately, we didn't have to wait. Alice came along 13 months after we were married, on January18, 1955. Alfred was extremely proud because neither his brother nor his sister had been able to have children. Lucille had adopted, however.

1954, Pregnant with Alice
Me, Alfred, Kathi, Aunt Anna, Anna May

Alice Melgaard – Born January18, 1955

Alfred and Alice

Christine, Alice, Victor, and Me

Summer of 1956, Prosser Park
The Californians in Prosser for their summer visit.
Back Row L to R: Uncle Jack and Alfred.
Middle Row: Me holding Alice, Kathi, and Aunt Anna "Shorty"
In Front: Anna May

Alfred had saved up $15,000, enough to build a house. We sold the little house for $500, and the buyers paid $800 to have it moved to North River Road. It had no foundation. Surprisingly the wood had not rotted. Since then, other owners have added onto it and one moved it a second time. It now stands on the corner of North Wamba Rd. and Merlot Dr., still white with green trim.

I helped shovel dirt for the foundation of our new house. The cement blocks were on their way, so I had to hurry! Mr. Heinz, the builder, said, "Boy, they must have really taught you how to dig in Russia!"

While our house was being built, we lived across the road in Aunt Anna and Uncle Jack's house. I really enjoyed the process of building our new home. They finished it in November 1956, a couple of months before Alice's second birthday.

1401 S. Missimer Rd., Prosser WA

Melgaard Dairy Farm
The corner of Old Inland Empire Hwy and Missimer Rd.

Fred arrived half a year after they finished the house, on May 23, 1957.

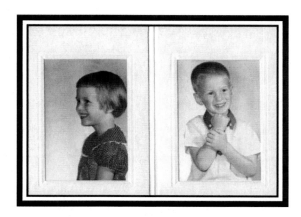

John came along seven and a half years after Fred, on December 28, 1964. Everyone was crazy about my little babies. I wanted four children. But, no such luck.

Lots of Grandparents

Uncle Jack and Aunt Anna visited every summer and stayed with us. My children called them "Grandfather and Grandmother Untch." Mr. and Mrs. Wilson were like grandparents to our children, too, the best anyone could ever have had. Their own relatives were jealous of the attention they gave me and my children. The Wilsons gave us things. "Don't tell the other relatives!" Mrs. Wilson would say.

At one point, my children wondered how they had so many sets of grandparents; the math didn't add up! They were smart children.

Becoming a USA citizen

I wanted to become a citizen, to *belong* and not just *be* in America. So, in the late 1950's, (from about 31 – 33 years old) I took night classes in American history. Alice was almost 5 and Fred 2 ½ when I went to take the test. Afterward, on December 16, 1959, I stood with 40 or so other people in front of Superior Judge Orris L. Hamilton of Prosser, at the courthouse in Pasco, and said my pledges. They gave us little American flags.

Pasco Courtroom Ceremoney

NEW AMERICANS — Persons receiving U.S. citizenship in Franklin County Superior Court proceedings at the courthouse in Pasco Wednesday are pictured during the ceremony with Claude Tomlin, immigration officer, who presented the group to Superior Judge Orris L. Hamilton, Prosser. In the group are: Manfred E., Bernd A. and Ralph M. Gaedeke, Elfride and Bruno E. Redweik, Ruth Eve Baumgartner, and Renate Merle Boltz, Germany; Manuel Diaz, Mexico; Renate Marie Boltz, Muriel Edna Campbell, Elizabeth M. Ferguson, Josephine and Cyril Simmonds and Sheila Sullivan, Great Britain; Anna Melgaard, Rumania and Miki Bowman, Frances E. McRae; Barbara I. Harville and Renee E. Hill, Canada.

Citizenship Ceremony
I am at table in front row fourth from the left

U.S. Citizenship Certificate
December 16, 1959 I'm 33 years old

CHAPTER 11

Back to Romania

After 1949, the measures aimed against the Germans in Romania gradually softened. In 1950 the Communist Party took over the farms, making them collectively owned. The Gypsies and Romanians got a sober awakening: they had to relinquish the property they'd taken, not to the Saxons, but to the State. And, if they wanted to eat, they had to work. Germans could now keep a portion of the crops they'd labored to raise. But, their quality of life progressed slowly; people who returned from the war or the slave camps were barely able to earn a meager living.

In 1956, the Saxons were granted "minority" status. As a result, their citizenship rights were restored and their homes returned to them. They found many of their houses in shambles, though, because of the lack of care and upkeep when the Gypsies had lived in them. They had to be extensively repaired at the owners' expense. Still, the Saxons now had hope. Tenacity, industriousness, and a sense of duty kept them going. They made improvements as well; gas was available, so they piped it into their homes. One could soon tell, by the condition of the houses, which ones had been reclaimed by their Saxon owners.

Visiting

I went back to visit Romania three times. Alfred would never go with me. "Why would I go where I couldn't understand what the people were saying?" He didn't want to be sitting in a corner alone while I chatted in Såksesch with everyone else. He always liked to be a part of everything and in on all the discussions and jokes.

First Visit

In the spring of 1967, when I was 40 and had lived in America for 17 years, I took my first trip back to Reichesdorf (now *Richiș.*) I brought 2-year-old John along with me. (The other two were in school: Fred was 10 and Alice 12.) This would be the first time I'd seen Mother in 22 years.

We took a plane, then a train. My brother, Hans, met us at the train station. At his first sight of me, he said, "You're so *old*!" So was he; he'd been only 14 when I left Reichesdorf and was now 35. As he drove us into the village, the first person I saw was my Aunt Regina, *right there*, walking by!

My feelings were such a mix. Everything seemed so familiar, yet strange. I felt happy and sad at the same time. This was my home, and yet it wasn't. What once looked so big was now so little! The river running through town seemed especially small, after living along the big Yakima River.

Things hadn't changed much. There were a few cars on the streets. People had phones, but no washing machines, which they all longed for. Everything else was still so *old*. My family's house, however, had been well taken care of and was in good shape. The Gypsies hadn't ruined it too badly when they lived there because my family hadn't moved out like other families had.

Mother, of course, had aged; she was now 70. My sisters, Sinni and Yinni were both still living in Reichesdorf – *Richiș*. Sinni had been only 7 when I'd last seen her. Now, all three of my siblings in Romania were married and had children.

Yinni lived in a house our father had built for her, with her husband, Andreas Weinrich, and their two children, Regina and Andreas.

Regina (Yinni) Untch and Andreas Weinrich on their Wedding Day

Sinni had married Heinrich Untch and had two children, Rosina and Anna (*Anni.*) They lived in a house they built themselves.

I had forgotten a lot of Såksesch, which frustrated me.

Hans had married Johanna Schass. (Her brother is the Herr Johann Schass on YouTube giving tours of Richiș.) They had Johann (*Hansi*) and Wilhelm, (*Willi*) and now lived in our family home.

John played with his cousins, Hans' boys. They seemed to have no trouble communicating. He mostly wanted to play by the river, throwing rocks off of the bridge. He liked the "plop" they made when hitting the water. That's all he remembers of the visit! The Saxon kids at the school were very excited about our coming and couldn't wait to see "the American boy," how he dressed, talked, and acted.

Johanna, Willi, Hansi, and Johann Untch 1972

We did some shopping in Medias and visited a different relative's house every day. They baked and baked and cooked and cooked to provide us with great feasts. You would have thought the Queen was visiting! The food tasted like *more:* I wanted more and more and more. However, my relatives had to sacrifice a lot - before and after our visit - to serve us these big meals. They'd had to save up their food rationings for a very long time. But, we couldn't refuse their generous offerings; it would have hurt their feelings.

Second Visit

On my second trip, I took Alice during the summer between her junior and senior years in high school. We set out for a three-week stay in Romania, but lost a week in Germany because of passport problems. However, this helped us brush up on our German.

For Alice, being in Reichesdorf - now *Richi* - was like stepping back in time: families still used outhouses, women washed clothes by hand, and people still drew water from their wells. Our hosts had bought special toilet paper just for her. They knew Americans weren't used to using pages ripped out of old catalogues!

May 1972, just before my second visit to Romania
Me, (45) Fred, (15) John, (7) Alice, (17) and Alfred

Alice got to meet all of my living siblings: her Aunt Yinni (*Yinni Tant,*) Uncle Hans (*Hans Onkel,*) and Aunt Sinni (*Sinni Tant,*) along with their families. My mother – *"Oma"* to Alice – was so glad to have met at least two of my children.

Some of the Saxon foods tasted very strange to my American-grown girl. She drank milk from a *Büffel* (a domesticated water buffalo.) Mother asked her, "Can I warm that milk up for you?" "No thank you!" Alice didn't think *warm* milk sounded good *at all*. The taste of water buffalo milk was strange enough as it was.

Another time, we had a little grappa, or *Poli* – the grape pomace brandy. Alice thought it was the *worst* thing she'd ever tasted. "Firewater. Rot gut. Just a drop of the stuff could ruin an entire glass of juice!" I guess it's an acquired taste.

For the most part, however, Alice thought the food was *incredibly* good. We had brought our hosts noodle makers and, consequently, they made us lots of tasty, chicken-noodle soup. The amount of baking the women did really impressed Alice. All the homemade, multi-grain bread spoiled her for the bread back home. Again, it was hard not to feel bad about the immense sacrifice of rations our relatives had made to make us comfortable and feed us so well.

When Alice asked Sinni what it was like to see her sisters taken away by soldiers to the Soviet labor camp, Sinni couldn't really remember; she had been so young, then. But, she did recall that our mother and the neighbor woman (who'd also had daughters taken away to the labor camps) would sit at their common courtyard wall and visit through a little window. They would talk to each other about their losses and cry together.

Our relatives talked Alice into having her hair done in Romania, which turned into an utter disaster. She explained what she wanted in English to me. I translated it into Saxon for Sinni, who then translated it into Romanian for the beautician. The woman gave her a permanent, but *much* too curly. Afterward, we spent many futile hours trying to straighten it. And this was just before she was to have her senior pictures taken. Not a happy memory!

The best thing for Alice on that trip was to be with her real, blood cousins (something she didn't have at home.) She had six teenage cousins there, all in one place and all around her age. They had learned a little English in school and just repeated everything until she understood them.

They walked her up and down the streets of Richiș, showing her all the buildings and places, and telling her stories about the people.

It also thrilled her to be with her only, *real,* still living grandmother. With the bits of Såksesch and German she picked up during those two weeks, she made a special connection with her Oma.

Third Visit

Me with my nephew Andreas Weinrich – Yinni's son

My third visit to Reichesdorf, I went by myself. By this time, my sisters were trading off keeping Mother: she lived with Yinni one week and Sinni the next. I wanted very much to bring her home to America. She would have done so well in Prosser, pulling all the weeds she wanted. All day long! But, she'd never come. "I would die on the way over," she'd tell me.

That visit was the last time I saw her. Mother died August 5, 1981 at the age of 84. I wish I had hugged her more. She was so giving and did so much for all of us. If we could be together now, I'd squeeze her for a long time.

Rosina Greger Untch Funeral, August 1981

Rosina Jr, and her mother Sinni, Yinni and son Andreas Jr, daughter Regina Jr and husband, Andreas Yinni's husband, Johanna and Hans

Romania Through the Late 20th Century to Today

Nicolae Ceausescu ruled in Romania as General Secretary of the Communist Party from 1961 to 1989. In 1965, the Romanian Communist Party took control of all business, politics, and cultural life. The RCP even controlled banks, insurance, and transportation. They rationed flour, oil, and sugar and allotted citizens only two days of electricity a week. They ruled the country by terror.

The Romanians forced many Saxon farmers into industrialized cities, undermining their ties to the native soil. They bulldozed down farming villages that Saxons had lived in for hundreds of years, condemning them to move to factory towns where they had no job skills; live in small, cramped apartments; and breathe polluted air. They could have no animals (pigs, chickens, etc.) for milk or food and no land to plant a few vegetables, making them completely dependent on a government that didn't care. The government also prohibited the German names of cities and stopped publicizing any German historic accomplishments in Romania. (This is why Reichesdorf is now called *Richiș;* Mediasch, *Mediaș;* Birthalm, *Biertan; and so forth.*)

Ceausescu and the Romanian Communist Party made life in Romania less and less bearable for the Transylvanian Saxons. The Germans yearned for freedom, wanting more and more to leave their Romanian homeland. In 1978, the government settled on an agreement regarding expanded family reunification: they allowed Saxons to be reunited with family members outside of Romania. Those who had relatives in Europe could now emigrate. Throughout these years, a quarter of a million Saxons left Romania for Germany. Finally, a revolution in Romania in December 1989 put an end to Ceausescu's dictatorship. When the Iron Curtain fell and the Romanian borders opened, most of the remaining Saxons streamed across them. There are less than 25,000 Saxons left in the homeland today.

There are only a few older Saxons left in Reichesdorf – *Richis*. Sinni and Heinrich, my little sister and her husband, had planned to stay, and had put *everything* they had to build up their home in Reichesdorf so it would last and be passed down to future generations. But, because of the mass emigration, there were no children or grandchildren left in Romania to give it to. When they tried to sell it, there was no one left to buy it. Everyone else was doing the same thing: trying to sell their home and get out of Romania. Finally, Sinni and Heinrich had to sell their house to the State for a mere 1,500 marks. She is so sick about this that she won't talk about it, even now. She and Heinrich moved to Cologne to be near their two daughters. None of my immediate family members live in Romania today.

Germany is Still Paying the Price for WWII

Sometime around age 65, I heard about a pension Germany was paying to all who had worked in the slave camps after the war. I applied, gathering all sorts of legal documentation proving I had served my two and a half years in Ukraine, plus worked various jobs when I was stuck in Germany for two years after that. Eventually, I was granted a small, monthly pension from Germany, which I still receive today.

Sinni Visits America

Sinni visited me in Prosser a couple of times. The first time, she came with Heinrich, their daughter "Anni," son-in-law Gary, and grandchildren Hans-Jergen and Wolfgang. Alice took a week of vacation so she and her family could spend time with them. We rented a 15-passenger van and drove *all* over Washington State: to

Seattle, (Monorail, Space Needle, etc.) the Everett Boeing plant, the Museum of Flight, Grand Coulee dam, Mt. St. Helens, the Ellensburg Rodeo, to name a few of the places. It was so nice to spend time with them.

I remember Sinni's husband Heinrich, after finally arriving in Prosser, didn't want to go to sleep. He was afraid he would wake up to find it had all been a dream.

I took care of the farm for almost 30 years after that, living as a widow. It was a sad day when I sold the last cow and stopped selling milk. But I was tired and there was still gardening to do. Sometime in the 1970s, I got some bean seeds from the WSU Experiment Station. They were nice bush beans and they produced almost all summer long. After trying them in the family garden, I planted extra beans in the field in front of the house. The kids and I picked beans all summer and sold some to the grocery store in town. It was a little side job that brought in extra money. But I loved hard work and didn't mind

Retirement

Alfred Melgaard milked dairy cows for most of his life and sang in the church choir for over 60 years. When he retired, we downsized the herd to eight cows.

During his 70's, Alfred suffered from cancer. First he had prostate cancer and then kidney cancer and died March 26, 1985. He would have turned 80 only 2 weeks later. Alice was 30, Fred 27, and John 20.

1983

80ᵗʰ Birthday

In 2006, Sinni came to Prosser again, this time for a month to celebrate my 80ᵗʰ birthday. She brought her granddaughter, Sigrid, her daughter Rosina's daughter. Alice took them to Mt. St. Helens again. This time huckleberries were ripe. Sigrid complained that she didn't have anything to put the berries in. Alice said, "I do!" and popped another handful in her mouth.

Sigrid also went to the Benton Franklin County fair with Alice, Steve and their friends Chuck and Kathy Brown. Sigrid got a henna tattoo and her mother was beside herself. However, the henna was gone by the time Sigrid got home.

Since then, Heinrich has passed away and Sinni and I have to be content to visit with each other over the phone. Each time, I insist on speaking Såksesch with her, so I won't forget my native tongue.

Family and Friends – the Rest of the Story

My sister, **Kathi Untch Drotleff** died in California from an illness on February 1, 1957, at the age of 37. Anna May was only 6 and was raised by a stepmother.

My sister, **Yinni Untch Weinrich**, and her husband Andreas, moved to Aschaffenburg, Germany. She developed heart trouble and died April 26, 2005 after a fall on her porch. Andreas died a few years later on December 26, 2009.

My brother **Hans'** oldest, Willi, got to Germany by paying a woman there to marry him. Once he was there, he divorced her (as part of the agreement) and sent for Ingrid, his true love in Romania. In the late 1970's, Hans got a work visa for Germany. He tried to get his wife, Johanna, to move there with him, but she didn't want to leave her family in Reichesdorf, so they stayed. After that, their youngest, Hansi, died at 17 in a swimming accident in the summer of 1974. Then, 9 years later, Hans himself slipped while fixing a broken sign high up on a building. He fell off the roof and died. Finally, Johanna moved to Germany to be near Willi, too late for the other two to enjoy a better life outside of Romania.

My sister, **Sinni Untch**, lived as a widow in Cologne Germany near her daughters, Rosina and Anna until her death in April 2016.

Georg Binder finally got to America and lived in Ohio. I heard about him through his sister and other friends. He has since passed away.

Regina Waffenschmidt Litschel (our grandmothers were sisters, so we were second cousins) met with other Saxon Romanians in New York, fell in love with one, and married him. He got cancer at the same time she was pregnant with their first and only child. He lived 7 more years. She never remarried. By working as a seamstress, (All us Saxon women were seamstresses!) she paid off the hospital bills and house. For one of her jobs, she sewed the linings of caskets for a funeral home. She bought a beautiful home and rented out the top floor. Also, she is very active in her church. Now, her daughter Kathy lives below her on the first floor of her house and helps her out. Regina and I are still close and talk on the phone regularly.

Mrs. Gertrude Kilkinney re-married. She and her new husband, Arvard Krohn, moved to Sunnyside. They raised currents and shared them with us. I made juice and snuck the juice into Kool-aide. But the children always knew. They could always detect "Krohn-berry" juice.

Jerry Johnson's wife died and he remarried.

Victor Wilson had a hernia that he refused to take care of. In 1960, he ended up in surgery for it and died on the operating table.

Christine Wilson moved to Walnut Grove Nursing Home in Grandview to be closer to her grandson, Walter. Still excited about going on road trips, she came to Alice's wedding in 1976. She lived to be 97 years old.

LSON — Funeral services for Mrs. Christina lson, 97, a longtime resident of Prosser, who ssed away Thursday, April 14, in Prosser morial Hospital, will be held Monday, April 18, 1 p.m. in the Chapel of SMITH FUNERAL ME, Grandview. Elder David Dordeaux of the osser Seventh-day Adventist Church will officiate. Burial will be at East Prosser Cemetery. e was born at Scotland, and when she was very ing, she with her parents came to the United tes, making their home at Streator, Ill., where e received her education. On Oct. 12, 1907, she, ss Christina Brown and Victor C. Wilson were rried at Tacoma. They later made their home White Bluffs, which is now the Atomic Energy ea near Hanford. In 1943, they moved to Prosser, king their home at 952 Brown St. Mr. Wilson ssed away in 1960. She continued to make her me at Prosser. She was a member of Buena ta Grange, and the Prosser Seventh-day Adven-t Church. She is survived by one son, Clyde of escent City, Calif.; three grandsons, Walt lson of Grandview, Clyde Wilson of Crescent y, and Merle Wilson of San Jose, Calif.; eight eat-grandchildren; three great-great-andchildren; two sisters, Mrs. Kate DeLano of coma, and Mrs. Alice Ennise of Illinois.

Aunt Anna and Uncle Jack both passed away in La Mesa, California: he first, then she moved to a nursing home and lived there until she died.

In 2015, at the age of 88, I moved into Sheffield Manor Assisted Living Facility in Prosser and used my free time to finish this book.

EPILOGUE

By heritage and culture, I'm German. By birth, I'm Romanian. By immigration, I'm American. I have now lived three quarters of my life in the United States: 18 years in Romania, 2 ½ in Ukraine, 2 in Germany, and 65 in America. People in Prosser have been very good to me.

Prosser is home and I have been happy here. I married who I wanted to and got to build my own house and garden. I've been able to do just what I dreamed of most in life: farm and raise a family. I have no regrets; I came out shining!

If there was one thing I could tell the world, it would be:

Stop fighting, people! War is a terrible, terrible thing.
It's the poor who suffer the most.

[However, because of WWII, Anna ended up in Prosser, made so many special friendships, married Alfred, and had three, wonderful children.]

Chapter 12

Family

Greger Families

Maternal Grandfather: ***Andreas Greger***, July 25, 1871 – July 1, 1941

Maternal Grandmother: ***Rosina Geltch***, February 25, 1871 – July 3, 1945

Mother: *Rosina Greger*, April 10, 1897 – August 5, 1981

Maternal Aunts and Uncles: Regina Nemenz, Anna, Friedrich, and Johann

Maternal Cousins:

From Regina: Regina Jr., Georg Jr., and Anna Nemenz

From Friedrich (Fritz): Gretel, Friedrich Jr., and Anna

From Johann: Johann, (Hans) Katharina, and Regina

Untch Families

Paternal Grandfather: *Johann Untch,* August 10, 1861 – August 6, 1920

Paternal Grandmother: *Katharina Schuster*, June 30, 1863 – January 8, 1913

Father: *Simon Untch*, August 6, 1890 – October 8, 1949

Paternal Uncles and Aunt: Johann, Adolf, Samuel, Friedrich, Wilhelm, Katharina, and Andreas
(plus *Sara,* Grandmother Katharina's orphaned niece, and an unclaimed half-sister by Grandfather Johann) Paternal Cousins:

From Adolf: *Adolf Jr., Johanna, Martin, & Katharina*

From Samuel: *Johanna (Hanni), Samuel Jr., & Johann*

From Andreas: *Renee (Untch) Notman*

From Sara: (my second cousins)
Anna, Regina, and *Johann (Hans) Waffenschmidt*

My Siblings

Katharina, nicknamed *Kathi*, January 29, 1920 – February 1, 1957

Regina, nicknamed *Yinni*, October 28, 1923 – April 26, 2005

Me, Anna, September 13, 1926 – August 30, 2016

Johann, nicknamed *Hans,* May 30, 1930 – August 10, 1983

Rosina, nicknamed *Sinni,* March 18, 1937 – April 29, 2016

My Children, Grandchildren and Great Grandchildren

Alice (Melgaard) Ard, January 18, 1955 –

Philip Ard, March 6, 1980

Tyson Ard, October 24, 1982 -- Great Grandson, Braden, May 2015, Tristan Sept 2016

Fred Melgaard, May 23, 1957 –

Christopher Melgaard, May 13, 1988

Cameron Melgaard, November 30, 1990

John Melgaard, December 28, 1964 –

Nieces and Nephews

From Kathi: *Anna May Drotleff Habetler –Kurt Habetler*

From Yinni: *Regina* and *Andreas Weinrich –Heidi and Harrold*

From Hans: *Johann (Hansi)* and *Wilhelm (Willi) Untch –Sylvia and Alex*

From Sinni: *Rosina (Untch) Waffenschmidt –Sigrid and Karl-Heinrich*

Anna (Anni) Untch Waedt –Hans-Juergen and Wolfgang

A Deeper Look

Mother's Siblings

Mother and her sister, **Regina**, were very close. When Mother was sick, Aunt Regina's visits really lifted her spirits. Regina married Georg Nemenz and they had three children, my Nemenz cousins: *Regina Jr., Georg Jr.,* and *Anna.*

--*Regina Jr.* met a Saxon man in Ukraine during her forced labor years. He had been blinded there in a coal mine accident, when dirt fell and buried him. Later, when freed from their service, they married. They had a good-looking boy. When widowed, she moved to Germany and lived with her son until she died.

--*Georg Jr.* married Katharina and they have a son and a daughter. They also moved to Germany.

--*Anna* died at nine years old of a burst appendix. My Aunt Regina always referred to her little Anna as *"Oingle mein,"* my angel.

Uncle Friedrich Greger was nicknamed *Fritz*. He took us to the dentist in Mediasch every year on his wagon pulled by his two horses, Otto and Bator. He married Margarete and had three children, my Greger cousins: *Gretel, Friedrich Jr., and Anna*. Uncle Fritz was deported to a USSR labor camp. At the end of his service, on the train ride to East Germany, he disappeared. No one ever found out what happened to him.

--*Gretel Greger* went to school with me. She married but had no children. She stayed in Romania until her death.

--*Friedrich Jr. (Fritz)* married my classmate, Lizzi, (Andreas Alzner's daughter) and had one son. They live in Ohio.

--*Anna* married Herr Froehlich and they had a boy and a girl. She moved to Germany as soon as the Iron Curtain came down in 1989.

Aunt Anna Greger married Georg Gross from Propstdorf. They met when she attended a party there. Georg came over to her and asked her if there was a girl for him in Reichesdorf. She said, "Yes! Me!" She was quite a character: bubbly and talkative. He was fairly quiet, a good match for her. He farmed, made shoes, and played the accordion. We had so much fun dancing to his music, especially on Christmas Eve. Aunt Anna wanted children, but they never had any. She would have gladly raised my sister Sinni. Georg was drafted into the German Army and never returned from the war. Aunt Anna moved in with her sister Regina, and died of a heart attack when she was in her 50s.

Uncle Johann Greger married Katharina. They had three children: my second set of Greger cousins: *Johann, (Hans) Katharina, and Regina*.

Hans married a woman named Regina and they had two children.

Katharina married and had a child.

Regina was so much younger; I don't know what happened to her.

Father's Siblings

My Father oldest brother, **Uncle Johann Untch**, nicknamed **Hans**, went off to America and married *Anna Waffenschmidt* (also from Reichesdorf.) They first lived in Ohio, then in Seattle, and later in Prosser. Uncle Johann (Jack) and Aunt Anna sponsored Kathi and me to come to America, gave us a home, and helped us find jobs. They had no children of their own, but became like parents to Kathi and me and grandparents to Kathi's daughter, Anna May.

My **Uncle Adolf Untch**, the next born, was quite a character, with a big, hearty laugh. His nickname was **Dolf**. He farmed, raising grapes and everything his family needed. He planted corn and climbing beans together. The beans would wind around the corn plants. He also grew cabbage, potatoes, and beets for the cows. He married a woman named Johanna and they had four children, my Untch cousins: *Adolf Jr.*, *Johanna Jr.*, *Martin*, and *Katharina*.

--*Adolf Jr.* married Anna and had two girls. He died while fighting in WWII.

--*Johanna* married and had two daughters. Her husband got sick and died. After the Iron

Curtain came down, she left Romania for Germany with her daughters and their families.

--*Martin* married and had three children, but he died early of an illness.

--*Katharina* married Herr Kloos and had two good-looking boys. They moved to the Drabender Höhe near Koln in Germany.

My **Uncle Samuel Untch** farmed and made barrels. He caught typhus as a child in second grade, and lost most of his hearing. He could hear some things, like thunder and pigs squealing. He could read and write some and was able to calculate to make wine barrels of different sizes.

Samuel married Sara and they had three children, my second set of Untch cousins: *Johanna*, *Samuel Jr.*, and *Johann*.

--*Johanna* (*Hanni*,) married and had one daughter.

--*Samuel Jr.* died in World War II at the age of 17.

--*Johann* married and had a daughter. He died of injuries from a brick wall falling on him when he was taking it down in Reichesdorf.

Uncle Friedrich Untch, nicknamed *Fritz*, caught typhus at six years old and lost all of his hearing. He and Samuel communicated with their own sort of hand language. He never married and lived in our family home his whole life. Mother took care of him until he died.

Uncle Wilhelm Untch, nicknamed *Willi,* moved to Germany, but because he had not changed his citizenship, he was drafted into the Romanian army. He quickly got his paperwork straightened out and never served. He married three times, but never had any children of his own. His first wife, Emma, had a son who died in the war. After he was widowed, he married Louisa. When she passed away, he married one last time.

~ 194 ~

Aunt Katharina was married for a few months before having a stroke. She lived only for a short time afterward.

Uncle Andreas left for Canada and worked as a winemaker. He liked to go to the horse races. Before heading out to one, he would say, "I'm off to feed the horses." He married Mary Knapitsch who had moved to Vancouver from Austria and lived with her brother Wilhelm. She and Uncle Andreas were married on March 25, 1933. They had one daughter, *Renee*, who still lives in Vancouver, BC.

Renee married James Notman on May 28 1960. They had two children: *Rosemarie* born June 14 1961 and *Andrew* born April 18, 1969.

My Grandmother Untch's niece *Sara,* whom she helped raise, married a man from Mediasch, Johann Waffenschmidt. They had three children, *Anna, Regina* and *Johann* (my second cousins.)

--*Anna* was a beautiful girl.

--*Regina (Waffenschmidt) Litschel* was the same age as Katharina. As told in my story, her life intertwined with Kathi's and mine during the most significant events in our lives. Today she lives in New York and we talk on the phone.

--*Johann (Hans)* was born in February of 1926, my birth year, but before the age cut off.

He was in the class ahead of me.

Keep making pies until you run out of pie pans!

Great Grandson Braden visits Oma

Anna's DNA test results

Anna's identity was always German. For hundreds of years, the Saxons kept to themselves, only marrying other Saxons. She knew she was pure German.

Son and daughter-in-law John and Mandy Melgaard had Anna take a DNA test. The results were quite different than she thought! To say Anna was surprised would be an understatement. This also led to a lot of speculation within the family, of course.

Part of the departure from pure German, was due to the fact that when migrating to Transylvania, more than Germans took Hungary up on the offer. One group was from the lowlands where there was some Scandinavian mixed in. The Southern Europe group would be the Romans/Italians who built roads within the Roman Empire which stretched all the way to Romania. Also, Romania was a crossroads for trade routes. People from all over came through the area to buy salt, a precious commodity and other goods.

All in all, the speculation and guesses amused the whole family in Anna's last years.

DNA Story for Anna (Untch) Melgaard

Ethnicity Regions	
Europe West	45%
Europe South	17%
Europe East	14%
Great Britain	10%
Ireland/Scotland/Wales	5%
Scandinavia	3%
Iberian Peninsula	3%
European Jewish	1%

My Three Countries – Afterward
by Alice Ard

August 30, 2016 was a nice, warm sunny Tuesday. My husband Steve and I were having an extension to our driveway poured. I was out taking pictures of the process to send to the grandchildren. That morning, Hospice was to evaluate Mom to see if she qualified. Her legs were extremely swollen and a wound had not healed in two months. Hospice informed me that Mom was eligible and we would sign the paperwork on Wednesday to make it official.

I got a call from the office assistant Beth Johnson at Sheffield Manor/Amber Hills about noon or one. She said that Mom had phoned her and said she was lonely. Beth said she would go sit with Mom. She called a half hour later and said that Mom's oxygen level was in the 50s. I told Beth to call the ambulance and I would meet Mom at the hospital.

I got to Prosser Memorial Hospital 45 minutes later. They put Mom on high flow oxygen and eventually gave her a diuretic to remove some of the liquid that was putting pressure on her lungs.

Mom was asking me questions, like "Where is my purse? I don't have any money." I told her not to worry; I would pay for anything we needed. Then she asked, "Is this a hardware store?

Where is Steve?" I explained that we were in the hospital. I noticed that her oxygen level was really low when she asked these questions. The ER gave her another breathing treatment and asked what I expected them to do. She was DNR (Do Not Resuscitate) and DNI (Do Not Intubate.) I told them that she was going into Hospice care the next day and Hospice wanted her pacemaker turned off. They checked with Mom's cardiologist and learned that her pacemaker would not try to shock her heart if it stopped beating. It did not have a defibrillator, so that aspect was fine. The ER doctor wanted to know if I wanted them to keep Mom overnight. They could put her on high-flow oxygen, but she would not have that when she went back home. I told them I would take her back to her apartment at Sheffield instead.

When we got back to Sheffield about 5 pm, Mom said she didn't want to eat. I rolled her in the door and went to park my car. I called my husband, Steve and asked him to bring me my pajamas, a change of clothes and all my medications, because I would be spending the night.

When I went back into Sheffield, Mom was sitting at the table, and they were bringing a plate for me, too. Mom didn't eat much, but we were still at the table when Steve showed up. Mom was so glad to see him. She had been asking for him for a couple of weeks, but he'd had a bad cold, so he had stayed away. She gave him her dessert.

After dinner, we went back to her room and I helped her get ready for bed. She had trouble lying down. She couldn't get comfortable. I tried placing pillows under her legs. Finally, Trina Franklin, one of Mom's favorite caregivers, came in and put more pillows under her head and rolled one up to put under her knees. Mom told me I could go sleep on the reclining sofa. A little after seven that evening, I was sending a text to my brothers when Mom said, "Alice, what are you doing?" Why Mom? Do you want me in there? "Yes." So I went in her bedroom and sat next to her. She took my hand. (This was very unusual, as displays of emotion were only for babies.)

Mom started moaning and I asked her what was wrong and where it hurt. She said nothing hurt and that she was just moaning. She also complained about being too hot, which is something I had not heard from her in several years. She was usually too cold. I took her comforter off, doubled it and laid it on the floor. I told her I would sleep on the floor for the night and hold her hand. She seemed pleased with that.

Michelle, her favorite caregiver, came in and took Mom's vitals. Her heart was beating 160 beats per minute and her oxygen level was in the cellar. She asked if I wanted her to call the EMTs. "NO!" I said. I told Mom it was not surprising that she was hot. Her heart was doing aerobics, but not the rest of her. Michelle left the room.

Mom was still moaning and I knew she was leaving. I told her, "Mom, I love you." She answered, "I love you too. You're a good daughter."

"And you're a good mom," I replied.

Then Mom said, "Help me!" And I asked what she needed help with, what I could do for her. She shook her head, slightly and said, "Help me!" again. It wasn't until the next day that I realized she wasn't talking to me.

Trina came back in the room with a nebulizer (breathing) treatment. She told another caregiver to call the EMTs. The caregiver left to relay the message. Michelle and the other caregiver came back in a little later. I verified with Michelle that no ambulance was called. Even with Trina's nebulizer treatment, Mom's breaths were getting farther apart.

"Mom, you are going to start seeing people you haven't seen in a long time." I told her. "Your old friends, and your parents and family will be there, too. They will be really excited to see you. Would you please give Aunt Kathi a hug for me?" By now, Trina, Michelle and I were all sobbing. And the breaths continued to grow farther and farther apart.

"And Mom," I said, "you will see a bright light. That's Jesus. When it's time, go to Jesus." She took her last breath at 7:45 pm.

I sat on the blankets on the floor of Mom's room, holding her hand with my left hand and making calls with my right hand.

Sheffield had to call an RN in to officially declare Mom dead. When the nurse finally got there, I introduced her to Mom. The death certificate will show she died at 21:19. Soon after, Don Howell came from the funeral home, and I introduced him to Mom. I was afraid they were all thinking I was crazy, introducing them to Mom. That's when I let go of Mom's hand, kissed her and went home. I didn't want to watch them move her lifeless body.

When I got home, I posted the following on Facebook:

"Mom crossed her last border tonight. She is finally free of her oxygen tube and physical maladies. Tonight she went to be with her family in heaven and with Jesus…"

We had planned to have a surprise 90th birthday party for Mom on September 10. She would never have agreed to a party, hence the need for a surprise. Well, scratch that party now. The Saturday after she passed away was in the middle of the Labor Day weekend. There wouldn't be time to get her obituary in the Prosser paper before the funeral. And people would already have plans for the long weekend. In talking with my brother John, he suggested having the funeral on September 10, the day we were going to have the birthday party. All we would have to do was change the wording on the cake.

So we had the funeral and people from all over the Yakima Valley and beyond came to her funeral filling the church sanctuary to overflowing. A great number of them took turns standing up and telling their Anna stories. The common theme was how incredibly hard-working she was, how clean she kept the milk barn, her sense of humor (including laughing at her own jokes), her gardening, canning, pickling, baking, cheese making, cider pressing, etc. After nearly dying of starvation after World War II, she spent the rest of her life making sure there was always plenty of food around.

What a legacy she left!

Obituary

Anna (Untch) Melgaard went to be with her Lord and Savior on August 30, 2016.

Anna Untch was born in a German (Saxon) community in Reichesdorf, Romania on September 13, 1926 to Simon and Rosina Untch. She grew up helping on the family farm where they raised grapes, flax, corn, beans, pigs and cattle. She enjoyed going with her extended family to work together in the fields. Many of the men from her area in Transylvania were forced into the German Army during WWII. After the war, Germans owed the Soviets war reparations, and thousands of young people from her area were shipped in box cars to slave labor camps in Ukraine. There they were forced to do hard physical labor, but were given very little to eat. After two and a half years, Anna was so emaciated that she was sent to East Germany to recuperate. Her sister was already there, and together, the girls escaped into West Germany. They were not allowed to return to their homes in Romania because they hadn't finished their 5 year obligation. They had an uncle, Jack Untch, in Prosser who spent over two years working on the paperwork to bring the sisters to Prosser. When they arrived in 1950, they saw fields and orchards full of produce and were reminded of home, but the hills surrounding Prosser were barren. In 1953, Anna married Alfred Melgaard and moved across the road to his farm, where they raised dairy cattle, alfalfa and corn silage. They bought more land and so began Melgaard's Dairy. A new house, barns and a garage were built to accommodate the growing farm. Many people purchased raw milk from Melgaard's Dairy until Anna retired in 1985.

Anna kept a very large garden until 2013. She preserved all the fruit and vegetables she raised. Her garden was always beautiful. One friend said she must have worked in the Garden of Eden. She planted extra green beans and sold them to the store in Prosser. Anna worked extremely hard, but was always happiest when working together on the farm. Anna was a long time member of the Prosser Presbyterian Church and the Buena Vista Grange.

Anna is survived by her three children, Alice (Steve) Ard, Fred Melgaard and John (Mandy) Melgaard, four grandsons, Philip Ard, Tyson (Corie) Ard, Chris Melgaard and Cameron Melgaard. She is also survived by great-grandson Braden Ard, several nieces and nephews, and two cousins.

Acknowledgements

Mom wanted to tell her story because she didn't think very many people knew about the atrocities in the Soviet forced labor camps after World War II. And she wanted to show that determination, persistence, frugality and hard work could get you through some extremely tough times.

I want to thank Mandy Melgaard for teaching me to just type whatever Mom said. I always wanted to correct everything, which stopped the flow of her story.

After I had typed everything I could, I didn't think the story flowed very well. In my defense, it was exactly Mom's voice. Any time I asked Mom how she felt when an event happened, she would shut down. Emotions were a sign of weakness to her.

When Mom moved into Sheffield Manor in Prosser, Ellie Fredricks was working in the office there. She was interested in Mom's story and was able to elicit much more information from Mom than I ever could. Ellie is the one who was able to put this into a readable story. For that I am eternally grateful. Thanks for giving up your lunches to talk with Mom, extract information from her, and put the story together in this format. Ellie researched and gleaned enough background information to additionally write a novel that links Romania during and after WWII with Prosser and the WSU Experiment Station!

The farm had been in the family since 1919, during which time, no one ever threw anything away, ever. There were five large barns and garages full of stuff, a large root cellar and a chicken coop in addition to the house. All had to be sorted and either sold or tossed.

I want to thank LaRinda Brown for helping with the gargantuan task of having an estate sale. You are an organizational wonder! I couldn't have done it without you. I also want to thank Jerry Lemmon, Jim and Stanley Gagner, Dan Brumley, Mayra Claro and Dulce Claro for your help at the estate sale. And thanks to Joan Gagner for making so many cookies for all the estate sale workers. Thanks to Jim Gagner for all the front end loader help and support throughout the process. And thanks to everyone who helped clean up the farm and made runs to the dump and the metal recycler. Thanks to Steve Ard for all the fruit picking, corn chopping and heavy lifting you have had to do over the years.